Understand & Seduce Men

The men's guide for women

From the first date to a happy partnership - incl. sex and dating tips.

Marlene corporal

CONTENT

Foreword

Men - they can be a real mystery to women. Between all the prevailing gender stereotypes, it's difficult to even keep track. The endless dating advice doesn't necessarily provide any more clarity either. This can almost bring one to the brink of despair when looking for a partner.

Does this sound familiar? Then don't despair, but read on here instead! You will learn to better understand men, how they deal with their feelings and what they expect from a woman. In addition, you will learn about the pitfalls of dating, which mistakes women often make and how you can avoid them. With many tips and tricks you will find out how and where you can meet men and win them over. Communication is the be-all and end-all and must not be ignored, just like the right approach to dating, but you'll learn all that in detail.

Often it is also already existing relationships that cause great grief, which is why I will go through common relationship problems with you and give you tips on how to deal with them. At the end of this book, you will also know what really makes a happy relationship and how to keep your prince charming by your side in a partnership. Furthermore, you will get information about spicy topics around sex life in a partnership and how to cope with different relationship models. Last but not least, you will learn what is important for your own personality development, because it should not only be about men, but especially about you! What are you waiting for? Get started right away and become an expert on men, partnership and your own self to create your own advantage!

Understanding men correctly

Before you can understand how to enter and lead a harmonious and healthy relationship with a man, it is important to understand men in themselves. Sounds easier said than done, doesn't it? Men are simple-minded. Men are and think straightforwardly. When men say something, they mean it.

There are countless clichés about both men and women. We live in the 21st century and yet the eternal battle of the sexes still continues. There are certainly numerous guidebooks, blog entries

or videos on the Internet that pretend to have cra-
cked a secret and to be able to explain the respective other sex. Only rarely does this lead to really
understanding each other better. The fact is, every
man is unique and by no means are all men the
same. But there are certainly differences in the
psyche of men and women, which are genetically
deeply rooted and even through evolution only
slightly balanced. Although everyone ticks quite
individually, one can certainly try to understand
how the opposite sex thinks, feels and acts. There
will, of course, be men who deviate completely
from these patterns, so it is best to focus on the
broad masses - heterosexual men who also identify as men.

HOW CAN WE UNDERSTAND MEN?

Let's think about this in practical terms - what can
you do as a woman to better understand the way
men think, act and feel? You need good powers of
observation, empathy and the ability to communicate openly with them. That, too, is easier said
than done.

Much starts with biology and the history of mankind. Why is it still mostly men who approach women and not the other way around? Why do men have a protective instinct by nature? Why do some men place such a high value on their careers? As I said before, there are simply differences between men and women that are biologically rooted. You don't have to be a history or biology nerd to understand why that is. Let's look back to the time when man lived as a hunter-gatherer. Even if meanwhile large doubts exist that women did not go also on the hunt for wild animals, it is considered as undisputed that above all the men were responsible for it. The man was thus - presumably - considered a hunter and provider, while the woman gathered plants and tended the children. Even if today's science takes a more critical look at this idea, it at least offers us a suitable explanation for many things. After all, this role model still holds up in many cultures today.

Apart from this evolutionary aspect, there are other biological factors that are still quite real today. The average male brain functions somewhat differently than the female brain. In addition, completely different hormones pelt our male counterpart, or at least in different concentrations. So you should first understand that the reason for how men fundamentally are does not come from a whim, but it is largely rooted in their nature, their biology. Now this may sound trite. Of course, there are many other factors involved, but in our daily lives, when dealing with other people, we quickly forget that we only have a limited influence on how we perceive our world, feelings, other people and our relationships. Empathy is the key word, because if you should ever be in contact with a man who gets on your nerves with his "typical male" behavior, remind yourself that there is not necessarily any malicious intent behind it. A lot depends on our ability to see into this person as well as on our ability to see into ourselves.

MEN AND THEIR EMOTIONAL WORLDS

In principle, it is probably true that the extent of the emotional world of men corresponds to that of women. However, you've probably often heard or perhaps even experienced yourself that men deal with their feelings differently. "Boys Don't Cry" is not only a well-known song by the band The Cure, but also a belief that seems to be widespread in many people's minds. Girls and boys cry about the same amount until they are ten years old. Why does this change with the course of one's development? Are men simply stronger, more resilient and less emotional? There may certainly be men to whom these traits apply, but that is by no means the rule; rather, our society teaches boys that they don't have to cry, that the have to be strong and ultimately take out their frustrations and all their problems on themselves. That can be incredibly stressful. Showing emotions, even allowing yourself to cry once in a while, shows real strength and is important for feeling balanced and at ease.

Use your knowledge of human nature as much as you can and try to feel how your counterpart, i.e. a man of your desire, someone you are currently dating or with whom you are already in a relationship, "works" in that respect. Is he rather cold on the outside and doesn't talk much about how he's doing? Or does he open up to you and let you share in his feelings? The chances that he will open up emotionally to you, a woman, are not bad.

In any case, you can often observe that male friendships tend to be interest-based and exchanges about feelings don't take up much space. As always, there are exceptions. And the extent to which a man is interested in you also plays a role in whether he wants to tell you everything in detail or not.

A man's emotional world can be just as complicated as your own. The decisive factor is how complicated your dealings with this person are. Someone who is at peace with his emotions and does not repress them may make it easier for you to understand him. However, don't judge the men who have their difficulties in understanding themselves. Yes, even women are not always in touch with their feelings, but this can be learned and changed. In this regard, many men are sadly victims of a society that dictates that they suppress an essential part of themselves. Once you understand this, it will be easier for you to better understand each man individually.

THE HUNTING INSTINCT

It may seem strange to come across the word "hunting instinct" when you're reading a relationship guidebook rather than a book on dog training. We have already talked about man's past as a hunter-gatherer. Beside it there is however a further point regarding the partner choice, which is still today of topicality. In this behavior, man is not so different from other animals. In the animal kingdom, there are many species in which the male courts the female and engages in sometimes fierce battles with rivals in order to be able to produce healthy offspring with a suitable partner. Humans are not quite so primitive nowadays, but the principle still works the same in many cases. Say: Woman selects, man can be selected. Men "court" their mistresses, women check, ask, check up. "That's completely outdated," you may now be thinking. Maybe you are one of those women who like to make the first move? Or maybe you're not. If you have any experience with online dating, you've probably already experienced that some men really force themselves on you, while you have to put most of them off. The principle behind this is exactly the same.

THE RESERVED AMONG THEM

Not every man necessarily carries this strong hunting instinct. There are many men who are rather reserved, do not know how to approach women or make contact, or simply want a woman who takes the helm and does not wait for a man to woo her. It is clearly crucial for a harmonious relationship that both parties complement each other well in this respect. So it's important to understand that men tick differently and not everyone wants to chase a woman, but you should first and foremost understand yourself. Do you like to make the first move? Is it not a problem for you to make an effort to meet a man who you like a lot, but who does not show any direct, obvious interest on his own? If you can answer "yes" to these questions, it's time to take a closer look at the more reserved type of man.

Depending on the degree of your own experience with women, there are men who have a hard time dealing with rejection and therefore avoid direct contact. Let's first note how you can recognize a shy man.

How to recognize shy men
• Pay attention to his facial expressions and gestures. Does he physically turn toward you or away? A reserved man will show his interest primarily non-verbally, namely by turning towards you and seeking eye contact. However, not everyone will seek direct eye contact. For some, this is simply too difficult, too uncomfortable. If he keeps looking over at you but doesn't approach you, chances are he's just shy but interested in you.
• What exactly is he doing with his body? Does his body language say caginess by folding his arms and trying to take up as little space as possible? Keeping arms and legs close to the body can be a sign of insecurity and shyness.
• Similarly, when a man hides his hands in trouser or jacket pockets. This posture is taken by someone to seek security and literally hold.
• What he does with his hands says a lot about him. If a man often plucks his clothes and hair, it can speak for insecurity and nervousness.

• If a man blushes quickly, this can also be a sign that he is rather shy. This is a completely natural and normal reaction of our body. Probably every-one has blushed in public in the presence of other people and knows that this can be very un-pleasant. This reaction cannot be controlled or hidden. So it's a sign that you're not leaving him completely cold!

These are all common characteristics of men who tend to stay in the background in the dating world. But not every reserved man is automati-cally insecure or lacking in self-confidence. Maybe a man will try to cover up or hide his insecurity by being defensive towards you, ignoring you, and being cold. How can you deal with this? Since turning on the hunting instinct doesn't work as easily for shy men as it does for others of their gender, you need to be a little proactive here. In the following, you will learn what you can do con-cretely.

This is how you deal with them

• Don't be too brash. A cheeky, very self-confident appearance may go down well with many men, but reserved men quickly feel cornered by it. Approach him with tact, establish friendly and polite contact to test whether he is also interested in you.

• Talk to him about his interests and hobbies. When you ask a closed person questions about his interests, he often opens up completely and becomes more approachable that way. If you express curiosity about his hobbies, sooner or later he will reciprocate, resulting in entertaining conversations.

• When it comes to communication, texting is your best friend. By sending a message rather than simply calling an introverted man, you give him some time to respond calmly. Many shy people find digital contact via messenger more relaxing than direct real contact or a phone call. So by responding, you convey understanding and respect.

• If you know that a man you would like to meet is shy, choose a casual setting for getting to know him. It can be an event or a visit to a museum. It is important that the place provides numerous external impressions. In this way, you give a man who is a little quieter enough time in between to think, to gather himself again and to find impulses for new topics of conversation.

• Finally, it is advisable to respond to his body language. If he hasn't made eye contact yet, just do so! You don't have to stare at him, in fact, you should avoid doing so to avoid making him uncomfortable. Signal to him in a subtle way that you find him interesting, so that he also gradually thaws out.

Basically, you should give him enough time and space. Keep things relaxed and calm. When a man returns your efforts, you will see that they were worth it.

MEN DO NOT LIKE TO TALK ABOUT THEIR FEELINGS

We have already talked about men and their emotional world. To better understand the gentlemen of creation as a whole, it is necessary to understand their feelings in particular. But this is not so easy when most of them do not like to talk about their feelings. Or do women want to talk about their feelings too often? The need for emotional sharing is certainly somewhat different for each person, but the opportunity to share and possibly seek advice from others is essential for all of us. The fact is that open, emotional conversations are good, provide clarity and more understanding of oneself and the other person, and make a relationship, of any kind, much less complicated. And this despite the fact that talking about feelings seems so complicated for some - quite paradoxical, isn't it?

In order to be able to talk about one's emotions, one must first and foremost be in contact with them and be aware of them. If, like many men, you have undermined and ignored this connection to your feelings for most of your life, it is extremely difficult to re-establish it at first. This is where some mindfulness and empathy are needed. For example, it can help to ask yourself every now and then throughout the day how you are feeling right now in this moment. What exactly do you feel? Are you calm, stressed, happy with yourself, disappointed, angry?

What good does it do you to even know how to talk about your feelings if we're just addressing a typical male problem here? Well, as a woman, you can help a man make that contact with himself so that he learns to talk about his emotions better. This can be done by simply modeling this for him. Initiate conversations about such topics on your own, but don't get too deep right away. For example, share when you are particularly happy or angry about something. Encourage him to empathize by asking questions. Ask him if he enjoys the food as much when you have a nice evening together in a restaurant. This may sound trivial, but in this way a man, as well as any woman, can learn to be more present and better understand what is actually going on inside him or her. If you are already a little closer, you can simply take him in your arms to signal that he doesn't need to hide from you. With a little luck, he will slowly thaw out.

As already mentioned, many male friendships are based more on common interests and hobbies than on deep exchanges about inner emotional worlds. It would be especially helpful for men who have difficulties with this exchange to talk about it more often with their male friends, because talking about it is best learned by talking about it more - logically. Try to be understanding if you find that a man has difficulty talking about certain things, and instead subtly encourage and inspire him to be more aware of listening to himself and sharing.

THE PROTECTIVE INSTINCT

We already know that the instinct to hunt is deeply rooted in the male world to this day. Perhaps you have also heard of the so-called protective instinct. For one thing, this kicks in when a man becomes a father and wants to defend and protect his baby as best he can. This is a logical and useful mechanism that nature has set up. But men want to protect not only their children, but also their wives.

"What good does it do me to awaken the protective instinct in a man?", you might be asking yourself now. After all, you're no longer a small, dependent child and you certainly already have both feet firmly planted in life. The thing is, many men just love to feel like they are needed by a woman. When they know they could protect a woman, defend her or help her in some other way, they feel useful and strong. So if you feel you are dealing with a man who gets some satisfaction from helping and protecting, go ahead and allow him to help you, even if you know full well that you could very well do something on your own. He offers to carry something heavy? Then feel free to let him do that too. You shouldn't feel guilty about letting him do things that you could do yourself. It's like give and take in this case.

As far as appearances are concerned, a feminine, not too tough appearance on your part is basically helpful to awaken a man's protective instinct. However, stay true to yourself and don't feel obligated to wear flowery dresses or long hair just to please someone. It is often advised to take advantage of the so-called childish scheme, and while it is certainly effective, it will do you no good if you don't feel comfortable in that role. Many men want to feel needed, but don't want to have to play the overseer. Nevertheless, it can be helpful for you to be aware of this in order to better interpret his behavior.

DIRECTNESS

Directness in the sense of communication is not bound to a gender, but one hears again and again that women would tend to express themselves more indirectly, while men would rather say plainly and clearly what they want. Of course, this is not true in many cases, because the world is not black and white and each person communicates in his or her own individual way. But as is so often the case, there is some truth in some clichés. Unambiguous statements with little room for interpretation are popular with men, so they like to use them themselves, but they also want women to communicate with them just as directly.

If you are in contact with a man and communicate with him, especially a lot via text messages, some misunderstandings are almost pre-programmed. Therefore, once again, a lot of tact is needed to read out or listen to exactly what he wants to tell you with his statements. Perhaps it is very difficult for him to communicate something directly. However, you interpret it as a clear statement and you are already talking past each other - quite annoying. If you notice that it is difficult to understand each other, practice direct communication yourself as much as you can. If you find this difficult, practice analyzing your own statements and keep asking yourself, "Can my statement be misunderstood?" if so, "How can I say what I want instead in an unambiguous but tactful and respectful way?" The difference in directness of communication is, unfortunately, often the reason between couples or people who are just getting to know each other why they clash. So you should know that many men appreciate directness and exemplify it themselves, because it saves you from one conflict or another.

HOW MEN FALL IN LOVE

Let's talk about how men fall in love. The development of infatuation from getting to know each other to the readiness for a relationship can be divided into four phases.

1. Phase: Physical attraction
For men it is indeed important that they first feel physically attracted to a woman. The reason is once again evolution, which thus caused men to seek partners who promised healthy offspring.

2. Phase: First emergence of feelings
The first feelings of infatuation arise that go beyond external attraction. As you get to know each other, your interest in the other person grows.

3. Phase: Matching the personalities
The extent to which the two personalities fit together is weighed up. Do both represent the same values? What about their sense of humor and hobbies? Does the other person have similar plans for the future? What similarities and differences are there? The focus here is on getting to know the potential partner even better.

4. Phase: desire for a relationship
Once it has been established that everything seems to be right on a personal level, the person is ready to enter into a relationship.

Unlike women, men tend to fall in love earlier, which is evolutionary. Women, on the other hand, place greater emphasis on personality at the beginning and put physical attraction further behind. In addition, women seem to analyze feelings more, which means that from their side the process of falling in love ends up in a relationship less often than from the men's side.

DOES HE FANCY YOU?

Many women find it difficult to answer this question clearly. Sure, you only really have one hundred percent certainty if a man tells you explicitly and also means this honestly. But we don't want to rush things at first and ask questions too briskly, because in the worst case this could end very unpleasantly. So what signs should you look for when you wonder if a man might be interested in you?

• He wants to see you often. If he frequently asks for meetings, suggests dates, and says how much he wants to see you again, that's a pretty clear sign that he's into you.

• He contacts you. You've just been on a date and now you have a new message from him: If a man is looking for frequent contact with you, he is certainly interested in you.

• He is looking for physical contact. If you see each other and there are small, seemingly random touches every now and then, or if he is obviously not afraid to be close to you, this is also a clear sign.

• He is interested in your interests. He listens to you attentively and asks questions about topics that may not interest him that much.

• He compliments you. Actually, a pretty obvious sign that he likes you, right? Pay attention to what he says. Even a small compliment says a lot.

• He makes compromises. For example, if he makes every effort to see you again quickly, even if he has to change his own plans to do so, this is a clear sign that he is interested in you.

• He wants to get to know your environment. If a man would like to meet your friends or family, he surely cares about you.

In principle, men, but also women, naturally want to show themselves from their best side in front of someone they are interested in. If you don't know a man very well yet, it can be difficult to estimate whether he behaves differently than usual. However, his body language and the extent to which he pays attention to you already say a lot. At the latest when he says it openly, you have clarity about it.

WHAT DO MEN LOOK FOR IN WOMEN?

This question, like many others, cannot be answered universally. However, from numerous surveys, studies and observations, a few points have emerged that are important for most men. What these are, I present to you in the following.

• A well-groomed appearance and the face.
The first thing we notice about a person when we first meet them, at least in real life, is inevitably their appearance. Men who are interested in more than just a flirt pay particular attention to a woman's face, her eyes and whether she has a well-groomed appearance overall. Even on hair or hands can fall their gaze.

• A beautiful smile.

A warm, inviting smile makes any woman seem more approachable and likable. When men weigh up approaching a woman they like, a smile she gives him is usually the deciding factor. This gives man a little more security and the fear of being rejected is less present.

• Naturalness.

You will certainly have heard that many men prefer women who radiate a certain naturalness. The term "naturalness" is very elastic here. Women should wear makeup, but not too much. They should have beautiful hair, but by no means extensions. She should dress stylishly, but woe betide her if she's too dolled up. My advice is to put on makeup, style yourself and act the way you feel most comfortable, because that's the only way you'll radiate true naturalness and, above all, authenticity. If you like to wear dramatic makeup, there will be men who like it, but many of them are suspicious of it because they think a woman wants to hide something in that way. In this context, naturalness is a word that is used in a completely inflationary way and ultimately does

not say much about a person. It's all about authenticity, which men value when they really want to
get to know you.

• Humor.

Every person with a sense of humor looks much
more sympathetic. It's not about a woman having
to crack jokes all the time to appear humorous, but
about the fact that she likes to laugh and can also
laugh at herself or his jokes from time to time.
Women with a good sense of humor don't take
themselves too seriously all the time - and that's
attractive. If you are on the same wavelength with
a man when it comes to humor, the attraction on
both sides is immediately much higher.

• Self-awareness.

Not every woman, nor every man, is naturally
blessed with strong self-confidence. Some even
find a little shyness in women attractive. But
above all, it looks attractive when a woman represents her own views and gives herself as she
pleases, without regard for the opinions of others.
A woman who knows her worth and goes through
life with a serenity has a very special effect.

WHAT ARE MEN NOT INTO?

You've just learned what men are into with women, but what puts them off?

• Constant self-criticism.

Yes, many women, but also men, have their little insecurities and problem areas, be it internal or external. However, it does not seem particularly attractive to men when a woman constantly talks condescendingly about herself. Some women hope to get some validation from him by telling her that she is beautiful the way she is anyway, but you should not look for this validation from a man, but within yourself. Accept your flaws (which in reality are usually none) and emphasize your assets instead. A woman who is at peace with herself looks much more attractive than one who only sees the bad.

• Constant dieting.

In connection with the self-criticism is that many women pay decidedly strong attention to their own weight and figure. It is of course exemplary if one does not let oneself go completely and pays attention to one's own health, but most men are rather put off if they want to go to a restaurant with a woman or cook together and she only has in mind not to eat too much or something too rich. If nutrition becomes a topic of conversation too often to an unhealthy extent, men often lose interest.

• Blasphemy.

Be it about an ex or other women: Blasphemous women do not look very attractive to men. To talk badly about others, to look for the blame and mistakes only in them, does not exactly speak of a good character. Behind this is probably also the fear that a woman who blasphemes about other people will sooner or later also pull over him.

• Bitchy behavior and nagging.

If a woman constantly wants to misunderstand a man's statements and reacts accordingly in a bitchy manner, this does not go down very well. Similar to blasphemy, the blame is sought only in the other person and bad intentions are assumed. In most cases, the problem is not with the other person, but with one's own attitude. It is appropriate here to take a few steps back from the situation, to ask oneself how something was actually meant, in order to react appropriately and calmly. Nagging as a bad habit can be unlearned and replaced by relaxed behavior.

What women fail at

When getting to know men or looking for a rela-tionship, there are some stumbling blocks that wo-men usually put in their own way. Much may be due to chance or factors over which we have no control, yet perhaps you too sometimes live in a dream world, with ideas that will never corres-pond to reality. So we miss opportunities, shoot ourselves in the knee by repeatedly falling for men who are not good for us at all, and are thus a lifetime in search of our Mr. Right. In this chapter, you'll learn what stumbling blocks there are and how you can get a different perspective on things.

YOU ARE LOOKING FOR A MAN WHO DOES NOT EXIST

"The right one will come along, he's out there somewhere". You may have heard this sentence before. Even if it is certainly true that every pot has its own lid, there is no such thing as the perfect partner, the "right one". Of course, it is good to have an idea of a suitable partner, because there are certain points that simply have to be right. You should be clear about your own values and know what is important to you in a partner. Of course, he should also be attractive for you, but it is not purposeful to limit yourself to too certain ideas, because we can lose the chance of a beautiful relationship just because a man may not wear the hairstyle that you like best.

Many women wish for a man that experts classify among the so-called "alpha softies": a man who is strong, self-confident and knows where to go, but who is also reliable, faithful and loving. Such wishful thinking is not very realistic, however, and already carries within it the impending disappointment we feel when we realize we can't find such a man.

THE MISTAKEN BELIEF THAT YOU CAN RE-EDUCATE A MAN

Women who end up with the macho type over and over again often live in the mistaken belief that they can change him. First of all, you should not get involved with a man who clearly has characteristics that are an absolute no-go for you, because the truth is that you can't change people just like that. If a person changes, it is only because the motivation to do so is intrinsic, that is, it comes from within the person.

So if you meet an attractive man who likes to go to parties, flirts with lots of women, or openly admits to having cheated in a relationship before, don't get your hopes up for change if these are things that turn you off. Some women desire to be "the one" for a man that he loves so much that he is willing to turn his entire life around and get better just for her sake. It can happen that men pretend to want to change, but in fact, conflict is bound to happen in such situations. So what to do instead? Being clear about your values and no-go's with a potential partner, and then clearly rejecting someone if they contradict our core beliefs, is the only sure way to avoid future problems.

THE FEAR OF MISSING A BETTER ONE

Sometimes it happens that women meet a great man who basically corresponds to their ideas and with whom everything is just great. If there were not certain little things that make him just not the "right". But as already said, there can be the perfect partner impossible. Instead, there is certainly for each person a whole range of potential partners with whom they could become very happy. In a world in which we can now establish contact with so many different men through online dating, it is increasingly difficult for us to thus commit to one of them, because every time we think that there could be another one with whom it goes even better.

Too much choice makes women very picky, usually too picky to find happiness in the end.

However, a never-ending search for a partner should not be the goal we strive for. The only thing hiding behind extremely high expectations is the fear of being disappointed. So if you also feel that this fear is getting in your way, try to free y-ourself from it by allowing things to happen when they feel right.

YOU LIKE MEN WHO ARE NOT GOOD FOR YOU

Or: You keep falling for a certain type of man with whom it will never end well. For some, for exa-mple, it's the macho men who have a very special attraction for them. With them it is exciting, whereas other men are boring. When a woman is used to being with a certain type of man, the habit settles in and they feel secure with what they al-ready know - even though this has usually ended in disappointment and pain. Also the disposition or what we are modeled have an influence on which men we are attracted to.

It can therefore be really difficult to break out of this circle. The only thing that helps here is to listen to yourself and question your own feelings.

Many women already feel at the beginning when it should not fit with a man, but ignore the feeling. You should respond to any concerns and rationally question the situation if you know that you are often attracted to men who ultimately disappoint you.

DESPERATE SEARCH

One problem that can affect any group of people is the frantic search for a partner. When one's own life seems too boring and monotonous, the solution is seen in a partner who is supposed to promise one happiness and adventure. It follows that some women overwhelm men with messages, cling to them very much and have too high hopes from the beginning. Sure, if you sincerely like a man and he doesn't seem to be averse to you either, you should show your interest openly and just don't hide it. However, if it gives the impression that you are desperately looking for someone, this is not only a deterrent for the man, but also not the way to a happy relationship for you.

In addition, some people fall in love faster than others, which also creates potential for conflict. Before you jump into the dating world, get a handle on your own life, have your own interests and hobbies, and above all, learn to get along well on your own. Think of a nice relationship as a positive extra, rather than a necessity to go through life satisfied. It's also perfectly fine to be actively looking for a partner, as long as you stay true to your principles and don't jump at every first opportunity. It can be helpful to have met several men before getting more serious with one of them. This will help you solidify your ideas of what you want and what is definitely out of the question for you. It also helps you learn to be more relaxed about things, since you can continue to look straight ahead after a date goes wrong.

Getting to know men - How to find the right partner?

Not every woman finds the perfect partner just like that. If you are still on the lookout for men, however, it may soon happen to you that you meet one by chance who blows you away. If you are not actively looking and are not in a hurry, this may be a comfortable approach. However, if you think that a steady partnership or other form of relationship with a man could enrich your life, it makes sense to think more concretely about the search and getting to know him.

BECOME AWARE OF YOUR INTENTIONS

The two most important questions you should ask yourself first are: "What are my intentions?" and "What do I hope for? So far, we have been talking about relationships, that is, solid partnerships that are of a longer-term nature. However, the possibilities are many and not every woman and not every man is necessarily always looking for a permanent relationship.

You could possibly just be interested in a casual relationship that doesn't have to last forever, but is just meant to enjoy some quality time together for a few months or a year or two. Equally popular is the relationship model of open relationships, where two people are a couple, but have a more casual relationship with each other, which usually allows them to still meet or become intimate with other people. The situation is similar with the so-called Friendship Plus, where the "Plus" usually stands primarily for non-binding sex. However, open relationships as well as Friendship Plus models carry the risk that one of the people will develop deeper feelings for the other person, which is quite likely to end in disappointment and a broken heart if this deep desire for a more solid connection is not reciprocated.

You may also want to find a real partner for life, that is, a lifelong, happy relationship. Not everything can be planned and you have little to no control over many things, but if you know that you are looking for something truly long-term, you will approach this differently. Also be aware that some things have to develop over time. For example, many relationships that started out as casual, no-strings-attached encounters have turned into true life partnerships. Of course, it is also crucial that your counterpart is equally clear about his or her intentions and that you share the same wishes in this regard.

MEET MEN - BUT WHERE?

This is a question that is often asked. You want to meet someone, you certainly know what possibilities you have, and yet you just don't know where to start. Theoretically, you could meet the man of your dreams almost anywhere you meet people, but the luck you would need is enormous. So, depending on your personality type, different ways and places to find a partner are more suitable than others. Let's take a closer look at them!

At the workplace

The workplace is a very popular place to meet other singles. In fact, according to a well-known dating site, more than half of all couples meet here. In the workplace, however, you should exercise caution when it comes to flirting. At a large company, this is much easier, since on the one hand you have more potential men to get to know and on the other hand it is easier to get out of the way should the affair not bring a happy ending. In the latter case, it is important to still maintain a professional interaction.

At the university or college

If you go to a university or college, of course, these are also great places to meet new men for dating. If you look around in your department, this has the great advantage that you are already interested in the same topics. Especially about this it is also easy to get into conversation, but in doing so you should still make it clear that you are interested in him as a person and not just in the subject matter or the upcoming exam that you are talking about. In addition, you can see each other regularly and arrange informal meetings, even if it's just for a coffee during the break. Apart from that, adult education courses are also an excellent way not only to learn new things, but also to get in touch with men.

Among friends and acquaintances
Meeting interesting single men through friends and acquaintances is both easy and effective. You could ask friends directly if they happen to know someone and then go on a nice first get-to-know-you meeting. It is also helpful to expand your circle of friends and acquaintances, as this maximizes your chances of meeting someone with whom you have a spark.

During sport

You value exercise and want a man who does the same? Then places like the gym or sports classes are ideal for meeting just such men. You already have a common hobby that connects you.

In the club

There are clubs for all kinds of interests. They can be for a particular sport, dance style, or community service. So if you are passionate about a particular cause and there happens to be a club for it nearby, see it as an opportunity not only to do something for your own interests, but also to get in touch with sympathetic men.

Classic in a bar

Is there a better place where people are more relaxed, sociable and, above all, flirtatious than in a bar? Hardly. A visit to a bar is the best way to get dressed up and put on a nice smile when you spot a man you like. If you are brave, go up to someone yourself. This can go down well and you have nothing to lose, only to gain.

Singles meeting

There are special singles meetings or parties that, as the name suggests, are for people who are looking for someone. Especially when you are new in a city, such meetings are a wonderful opportunity to get in touch with other people, especially because you can be sure that all the men there are also looking.

At concerts

If you are passionate about music, concerts are another suitable opportunity to strike up a conversation with men. In any case, one advantage: you share the same or at least very similar taste in music.

When dating online

Online dating is becoming increasingly popular. Especially if you find it difficult to get into conversation with men in real life, online contact can offer a good alternative. In addition to the classic dating platforms and special dating apps, there are numerous ways to establish contact. There are even couples who met through online games.

Nothing is impossible here. Even though there are certain stigmas around online dating, you shouldn't let them scare you away and give it a chance. Be as authentic as possible and see where the journey takes you!

HOW TO FLIRT PROPERLY

What is flirting actually? You think you know, but in any case it's not what you see in Hollywood movies. Flirting is like a non-committal, spontaneous game that can take place anywhere time, place and opportunity allow. Above all, it should be fun and doesn't always have to mean that the person is looking for closer contact or even a permanent relationship. Nevertheless, getting to know each other often starts with a flirt. You don't enter into any obligations, which means that you or the other person can end the situation as soon as you no longer want to.

But how do you flirt "properly"? If it's like a game, there must be certain rules. On the Internet and elsewhere in the world, there are a lot of tips circulating, many of which are really outdated. "Seeking physical contact" or "sex sells" doesn't always work or can backfire in the worst case. I would like to give you a few tips as a basis with which you can do practically nothing wrong.

1. Be authentic.

You already know that it pays to be authentic. Flirting is all about being yourself at that very moment. So don't think too long about how you can be as charming as possible, because the best way to do that is not to think about it. You don't even have to say anything to flirt with someone. A look or a smile already says a lot and you don't have to pretend at all.

2. Don't take yourself too seriously.

The feeling of being very small in a world with all these people who have their own problems and for whom their own life is just as important as yours is for you can sometimes be quite overwhelming. This feeling can help you not to take yourself too seriously and too important. Especially when flirting, it is important to have fun and not to worry about what will happen if the other person does not react as we had hoped. Somewhere in the world a person is constantly flirting with another person and only in the rarest of cases does it turn into something worthy of a movie. Think about it and, if necessary, see a failed flirtation as an exercise.

3. Stay loose.

This point follows on from the previous one. If you don't take yourself too seriously, it's much easier to stay loose. But that's sometimes easier said than done. If you ever have to take a failure, it's important that you don't let it deter you. It might discourage you from trying again in the future, and especially if you see a man you particularly like, that would be annoying after all. Just see it for what it is - a relaxed, totally non-committal game.

4. Be brave.

The most direct way to pay a nice compliment to someone or to talk about something that has caught your eye is the best and most effective way to sweeten the day for your counterpart. For example, if you notice that a man has a nice smile, you can say it straight out if you honestly think so. Don't hope for anything, you only have something to gain if it turns into something more.

5. Forget all the tips.

Yes, maybe also the ones I have just listed. Above all, forget everything you've ever been told about proper flirting. Too many tips and thoughts that are floating around inside you before or during a flirt are more than counterproductive. They block you in your authenticity and spontaneity, although it is precisely these things that matter. As in many other matters, the same applies here: The proof of the pudding is in the eating!

CREATE A POSITIVE AURA

If you radiate positivity and joie de vivre, your chances of having an equally positive effect on a man are much higher. A positive charisma can generate spontaneous sympathy without having to know a person better. This can bring you success not only in terms of meeting men, but also in general with all the other people you come into contact with on a regular basis. With a positive attitude and charisma it is simply much more pleasant to go through life. So that you can also benefit from it, here are a few helpful tips.

1. Practice self-love.

Positive charisma always starts with self-love and self-acceptance. You can achieve it by focusing on your strengths rather than your weaknesses. What qualities do you really like about yourself? Focus on them completely. Being aware of your strengths makes you more self-confident and you get to know yourself better. Internalize the belief that you are good and unique, just as you are.

2. Accept other people in their uniqueness.

It doesn't stop with self-acceptance, but continues especially when it comes to acceptance for other people. Perhaps you too sometimes catch yourself unconsciously judging someone and thinking something bad about them, even though you don't know that person. When we treat others this way, we also treat ourselves this way or assume that other people will judge us just as badly. If you free yourself from this thought and tell yourself that you, as well as everyone else, are fine the way they are, you will immediately radiate this positivity outward. It also follows that you should not try to change other people. This is a hot topic especially in relationships and, as mentioned earlier, a common but false assumption especially among women that they can change a partner.

3. Pay attention to your posture.
Your posture not only massively affects the effect you have on other people, but also how you feel about yourself. Try it out by walking around with your posture bent and your arms crossed. You're sure to feel pretty lousy - insecure, small, just bad. And then you will walk through the world upright, with your eyes always turned forward, open and with a friendly smile. The same situation will suddenly feel completely different, and you've brought this about entirely through the power of your own body language. Also, pay attention to the people around you, how they affect you with their respective postures and how they in turn react to you. Physical posture is one that is often underestimated when it comes to how our inner posture is.

4. Use your voice and speech consciously.
We know by now that language influences our thinking, and not just insignificantly. It therefore makes sense to pay attention to a positive choice

of words for a positive aura, both when you speak to yourself internally and when you do so with others. Try to replace the word "must" with "may" sometimes. In this way, you give yourself and others a choice that immediately creates a positive basic feeling.

The voice is also a powerful tool to hone your charisma. If you are interested in this topic, you can attend courses or simply practice at home by reading something aloud and paying attention to the effect of your own voice.

5. Don't conform on the outside.
This means that in terms of clothing, hairstyle, etc. you should not try to meet the expectations of others. Of course, your style also has a certain effect and other people may or may not like this style. However, what makes you look incredibly appealing is if you feel comfortable with your appearance. You won't get anything out of a fancy hairstyle if you feel like it never fits right. It's the same with clothes that make us look unflattering or make us feel like we're not ourselves.

PARALLEL DATING

Dating several people at the same time until it eventually gets a little more serious with one of them is not that uncommon today, even if many wonder if it's even okay. No-go or in keeping with the times? The decisive factor here is the right approach.

These are your advantages
First of all, we can state that it can be advantageous to keep several options free. This is especially true for online dating, because it makes sense to make several contacts at the same time. It is uncomplicated and saves you a lot of time compared to immediate real meetings. You should send as many requests as possible, as this increases your chance of receiving positive feedback. However, make sure that your messages do not sound like "copy & paste", but always have a personal reference. With online dating, you have the great advantage of being able to reach a large number of men, which means that the probability of finding the man of your dreams is very high. So even if you can save a lot of time at first, you should still

be prepared for the fact that the search will not be absolutely effortless if you really want to meet interesting people.

A plus point of parallel dating is that you get to know your own desires better and your ideas become sharper. You know what you expect from a partner and which characteristics of a man, on the other hand, do not suit you. You could also compare this form of dating with the trial and error principle - the more you try out, the more likely it is that you will eventually find something suitable.

Furthermore, you have a direct comparison between all your dates. Of course, only a real meeting will show to what extent you harmonize with a man, and several meetings with different people allow you to weigh the extent to which the chemistry is right. As long as the mutual acquaintance is still at the beginning, there is nothing wrong with parallel dating of several people, but you should not play this game too long. Otherwise, the contacts will remain on the surface forever and you will prevent yourself from getting to know someone more deeply if you keep too many options open for too long.

At what point does it become problematic?
You should definitely talk openly with the people involved about the fact that they are not the only ones you meet with when ...

• ... you notice that feelings and the desire for more arise in one of them. In that case, it's only fair to explain your situation and your intentions to your counterpart, so that the person can decide whether it's (still) okay for them.

• ... you have become intimate with someone. Unless it has been clarified in advance that neither you nor your counterpart are looking for something non-committal, you should also address the topic openly in this case. In this way, you prevent the person from possibly feeling deceived after he or she casually learns about your contact with others.

So you see, honesty with yourself and all the people involved is enormously important in parallel dating. Also, if you find out that a man you are dating is keeping several options open, even though you are seriously interested in him, you should seek the conversation. The longer such

games are played, the more painful it will be in the
end, so think carefully about how far you want to
go.

He does not want a relationship - What now?

You have now met a great man, all your efforts have (almost) paid off! Maybe you are already head over heels in love and think to get the same signals from him. You look for the conversation or ask him how it stands around another meeting and ... out is the dream, if he tells you that he just wants to be friends with you or gives another reason. The fact is, he doesn't want to get into a relationship with you. You have to let that sink in first, but also encountering rejection is simply part of the partner search, because at the end of the day, everyone who is looking for a partner wants one like that, with whom they can be happy. And sometimes you have to be honest enough with someone and yourself to say that you'd rather not try if you sense it's not a good fit.

In most cases, this decision is unchangeable, which means that it makes no sense to try to change his mind. Desperation can't change anyone's mind and if it does, the person who lets himself be changed surely has his own problems or even feels confirmed by letting the other person beg. So if you find yourself in such a situation right now or sometime in the future, make sure that there is nothing concrete you can do about it, except to face it with acceptance. It usually makes sense to try to distance yourself from the man in order to change your mind and get over him, but this is often not the end of the matter.

HE WANTS FRIENDSHIP INSTEAD

In many cases, people who are dating, after some time, not romantic, but friendly feelings tune in. However, sometimes you think you are in love, but after some time you realize that the feeling does not really go beyond friendship. "Shall we stay friends?" is a sentence that you may have heard once during a breakup or said yourself, but no one really wants to hear it. The same is true when this phrase comes up in the dating phase. If you find yourself in this situation, but you yourself had the desire for more, it will certainly take some time until you have finally digested this. Whether you can or want to be friends with a man after he rejects you is entirely up to you. Let some time pass, concentrate on yourself and your hobbies and if you still have the feeling that you want to be friends with him because you find the contact with him enriching even on a purely platonic level, then go ahead and accept the offer of friendship or leave it alone if you don't feel like it.

HE DOES NOT WANT TO LOSE YOU

Perhaps his refusal to you will also be accompanied by the saying "I don't want to lose you". This can have a similar meaning as the expressed desire for friendship. However, it can also mean that he does not want to commit, but likes you and can possibly imagine an open relationship, friendship-plus, etc..

Again, the important thing is: What do you want? If you are looking for a serious relationship, but a man expresses that he does not want to enter into one with you, then you should not just let yourself be fobbed off. Also, don't settle for less if there's a secret hope lurking inside you that he might change his mind, because that usually doesn't happen. It can feel like a tricky situation, but if you don't want to settle for anything less than a relationship, it's best to let this man move on.

Communicate with him properly by text message

Communicating with each other via text message is practically a matter of course today. In addition to the classic, albeit somewhat outdated text message, there are now numerous messengers and apps for cell phones that make communication between two or more people quick and uncomplicated. However, virtual communication has its dangers, since essential aspects that we perceive in real contact with someone are omitted: the voice, the tone of voice, body language and facial expressions, eye contact and many other details. So when it comes to flirting or getting to know someone by message, a great deal of tact is required to avoid sending the wrong signals or misinterpreting messages yourself.

Online dating in the initial phase consists almost exclusively of written contact, which means that especially the initial contact can decide whether you will get to know a man or not. But even if you have already met someone, the virtual contact usually does not stop. After all, to arrange a meeting, it does not necessarily need a phone call, although this is a bit more personal, but also a matter of personal preference. It's not uncommon for people to clash in purely digital communication because they misunderstand messages or even want to misunderstand them, don't question their own behavior, and don't address problems openly. If you're thinking about flirting by message, you may also have some content-related questions buzzing around in your head, because it's not just the "how?" that matters, but also the "what?". This short chapter is about exactly that.

THE FIRST CONTACT

If you are looking for contact with a man for the first time in online dating, it is sometimes not so easy to find the right words. To increase your chances of getting a positive response, here are some tips to make this first contact easier.

• Compose a personal message.

If you take a look at his profile and notice something exciting, talk to him about it. Open-ended questions are always well received and make it easier for him to respond to your message. For example, do you see that you share a hobby? Or does he tell you in his profile that he likes to travel? Questions about such things are a great conversation starter.

• Be friendly, pay attention to form.

A message that does not come across as scribbled immediately creates a more positive impression than one that is full of spelling mistakes. Also, a nice salutation and a closing seem polite and show respect for the person who is being written to.

• Make him curious.

You can tell him a little bit about yourself to get him interested in you. If you share a hobby, don't just ask him about it, but casually mention what you're interested in. This will spur him to want to learn more about you.

• Be humorous and positive.

A humorous message, which may include a funny anecdote from your life, is very well received. In any case, don't formulate your message too dry or serious, because that doesn't exactly contribute to a relaxed get-to-know-you.

- Remain discreet.

Too intimate questions are not a good way to start. Furthermore, you're much better off with a shorter message than with a page-long text. Your conversation partner will feel less pressured and, above all, less taken off guard.

- Show sensitivity.

You don't yet know how the man you want to write to communicates at all. So show sensitivity, give him time to answer, but above all time to get a mutual feeling for the respective communication style of both of you.

When should you write to him?

The beauty of communicating by message is that it doesn't matter when you write a message, because the other person is not obliged to reply immediately. However, if you don't want to wait forever, it may be a good idea to write to him in the early evening, as he will most likely be done with most of his daily tasks and will have time to devote to your messages. At this point it is also important to mention that you should not overwhelm him with messages if he does not respond immediately. The fact that he doesn't write back right away doesn't have to mean that he doesn't feel like talking to you or that he wants to ignore you, but can have completely different, harmless reasons.

YOU ALREADY KNOW EACH OTHER A LITTLE: HERE'S WHAT HAPPENS NEXT

In the meantime, you have met a man and perhaps already met him. In any case, contact via text message continues, which is crucial here. You've already been able to tune into each other's communication style quite well and are now in regular contact - it's going well! But still, this may raise some questions for you, so I'd like to say a few general words on the topic of text messaging communication, regardless of your current state.

Keep the conversation going
Don't let him play the solo entertainer, but make sure that your exchange remains lively. Initiate the conversation and don't just expect him to keep coming up with new topics and writing to you,

because this shows that the interest is not just one-sided.

A classic topic and conversation starter is the question about how his day was. It may sound a bit trite and he may only answer briefly and succinctly, but keeping each other up to date creates closeness, even if you haven't seen each other yet or can rarely arrange meetings because of the distance. Sharing your life with each other is not only nice, but also relieves the stress of everyday life. But be careful: You should not be a shrink for each other, so keep the topics rather positive instead of venting too much about negative things with him.

Shared interests are always a good occasion to talk about them. But what is perhaps even more exciting is to ask him something about hobbies and interests that you do not necessarily share. This is another way to show your interest and get to know him much better.

But when is it enough? Hanging out on your cell phone all day and sending each other messages may be fun for a while, but there will come a point when you no longer have much to say to each other. So feel free to end the conversation when you feel you've reached your zenith. If you leave a conversation in a positive mood, you leave him looking forward to the next contact with you.

How long should you wait to answer?

This is probably a frequently discussed question. The assumption that you have to wait three days after the first contact before you get in touch is also persistent. But even in normal chat with him, you certainly wonder how long you should wait until you answer him again. 'Do I seem desperate if I write back right away?' or 'Does it seem like I have nothing else to do but wait for him to reply?" are questions you may have asked yourself directly or indirectly. Some even make a real game out of it and feel attacked when they are supposedly ignored for too long. A well-intentioned advice at this point is: Behave honestly and show honest interest in him, if you have this. If you want him to pay some attention to you and not make you squirm unnecessarily, then behave the same way yourself. This makes it much more likely that he will voluntarily behave the same way towards you. Not ignoring his messages just to keep him waiting is a sign of respect, and mutual respect is an important foundation for relationships of all kinds. If you're busy and get a message from him that isn't answered in a sentence or two, write him that you'll get back to him later. This will show him that you are conscientious and he will look forward to a more detailed reply from you.

Use emojis

Admittedly, squeaky yellow emojis are not to everyone's taste. From the simpler form using punctuation, emojis have also found their way into everyday written communication via messenger apps in pictorial form. The big advantage of them is that you can convey a feeling much better than via text alone. Details that would otherwise be completely lost can be emphasized in this way. Of course, you shouldn't overdo it, but be aware that you can also use emojis to support a statement in a certain way or give it a completely different meaning.

Shares content with each other

Photos from your everyday life, your favorite song or an exciting news article from the Internet -

these are also things that can bring you closer together. A lot is possible these days via messenger apps, so take advantage of this opportunity. In addition, you create new conversation incentives with such content, which keeps the contact exciting and enriching. Again, though, less is more, so don't overdo it. Because we like to write to someone on the go, we don't always feel like dealing with more content.

HE NO LONGER REPORTS

Sometimes, unfortunately, it can happen that someone, out of the blue, doesn't contact you from one day to the next and doesn't respond to your messages. In this case, you should first remain calm, because this behavior can also have good reasons, as long as it does not continue over a long period of time. On the other hand, especially in times of online dating, the inhibition threshold regarding so-called ghosting has decreased more and more. That is, a person breaks off contact with someone without justification, as this seems more convenient and easier at the moment than explaining oneself.

The only way you can find out what the real reason for his absence is by asking him. Write him a message, but be sure to refrain from using a reproachful tone, as this will decrease the chances that he will write to you at all. That's all you can do in this situation. If he doesn't reply to this message at all, you should put the matter with him to bed, because he has obviously lost interest and this will almost certainly not change. Sure, it's unfair of him to act this way, but if it happens, you shouldn't waste any more thought and energy on it. If the contact hasn't lasted long and you haven't met in person, it should be a situation you can handle well.

THE CONTACT IS ONE-SIDED

You constantly initiate new conversations, want to find out more about his interests and want to meet with him, but hardly anything comes back from him. It can also happen that the contact decreases slowly but steadily over time and he contacts you less and less often. Here, too, you can ask specifically, but in a friendly manner, what the reason is. It is possible that there are understandable reasons for this that have nothing to do with you. The other possibility is that he simply loses interest. The situation is similar to the previous point.

If you cannot clarify the matter with him, there is no point in continuing to chase him. You should then clearly tell him that you are no longer interested in contact and end the story.

You would like to meet

So you are in contact with a man and you maintain a lively exchange. Sooner or later, the desire for a first meeting will usually arise - quite exciting! But what should you clarify beforehand and what do you do if he doesn't ask you out? These are the questions that this chapter will deal with.

YOU SHOULD CLARIFY THIS BE-FORE THE MEETING

1. What are your intentions?

You don't have to go into detail, but you should still roughly clarify what you actually want and hope for from this date. Do you both want a committed or open relationship or just some fun? If your intentions are fundamentally different, you should rather refrain from a date, because you will not come to a common denominator. If you or your counterpart are open to everything, however, a good relationship can certainly develop if you find that you are suited to each other.

2. How much time do you have for each other?

It can't hurt to clarify in advance how much time you want to take for the date. This prevents expectations from being disappointed, for example, because one person has to leave early while the other would have liked to stay a little longer. So, if you are planning something for the afternoon, feel free to ask if you want to go out for a meal or a drink afterwards. It is advisable to plan several small activities, as it will then be easier to interrupt the date if you or both of you realize that things are just not going well.

3. Do you have any principles for a first date?
For example, for some it's a no-go to get intimate right away on the first date, while others are open to many things. Both are fine, but it would be better if you talked about such principles before the date. This will also take a lot of pressure off each other if you know what to expect and what not to expect.

4. What happens if the date is a flop?
Of course, it helps to go into the first date in a positive frame of mind, but you should still ask yourself what you will do if it turns out to be more of a bust. This means that you should not resort to nasty dating tactics like ghosting or benching. Ghosting is the abrupt, immediate break off of contact without justification, while benching is a term for the behavior when someone is literally left sitting on the long bench, although there is no serious interest from the other person. Instead, make it clear that no matter how the date goes,

you want to be honest with each other afterwards, because this will save you a lot of discomfort.

HOW DO YOU ASK FOR A MEE- TING?

Asking a man for a date is not difficult at all and sometimes you have to take the initiative yourself if nothing came from him for the time being. In principle, you have two options: You ask him directly or indirectly for a meeting.

1. The direct approach

Asking directly for a date works well, especially via text message, since you give him some time to respond. Since many men don't expect female initiative, you don't catch him off guard here. You could choose a casual conversation starter and ask about his day before asking an open question about getting to know him in person. If he responds positively, you can also go straight into a proposal for the date and a specific date. It takes some finesse to guess whether he is serious about meeting you. So if a specific date doesn't suit him, just ask if he would like to do one of the activities in principle, and let him choose a day or suggest another one.

2. The indirect approach

If you don't want to be quite so offensive, it might be a good idea to give him an advantage so that he suggests a meeting of his own accord. For example, you could say that you would like to go to that nice café in town or to a certain exhibition, but so far you haven't found a suitable companion or the right opportunity. If he is interested in you, he will take the chance and ask you if he can accompany you.

Your first date

It's done, the first date is coming up and you are certainly a bit excited. You may have a lot of questions, concerns, but also hopes, so it is advisable to take precautions so that you or both of you are not completely lost just before the date. In the following, you will learn tips and tricks that will simplify the planning before the date and also the meeting itself.

WHAT IF HE CANCELS?

You should not assume the "worst case", but it can happen that someone cancels a meeting at short notice. The shorter the notice, the more stupid it is for you, of course, because you assumed that you had agreed on a fixed meeting, and then you find yourself without a plan. He may give you a lame excuse and claim that it was an emergency or that he was ill. If you think there's something fishy about it, it's almost certainly an excuse and he probably wasn't seriously interested in meeting you in the first place.

However, there are also situations that are plausible and for which you have to cancel a meeting sometimes. Whether he is not secretly lying to you and honestly wanted to meet with you, you can tell in most cases by the fact that he immediately suggests an alternative date and affirms how much he would have liked to go on this date with you. If he actually has an understandable reason for canceling the meeting, he will provide you with a background story explaining the situation and probably try to keep in touch with you throughout the day anyway. Your gut feeling is basically a good indicator of his true intentions with you.

SUITABLE PLACES AND ACTIVITIES FOR A FIRST DATE

First, let's keep in mind what makes a good place to date and which ones you should rather avoid.

You should choose a place ...
- ... where you both feel comfortable and have fun. In a neutral place, no one has a home field advantage.
- ... which offers enough to talk about. This makes it far less likely that there will be unpleasant pauses in the conversation.
- ... that fits your or your personalities. So you feel comfortable and the meeting will be remembered.

Places you should rather avoid
- At your place or at his place

Choose a neutral place for a first meeting. You may think you already know the person a bit, but a meeting in your own four walls is rather unsuitable for a first date.

• Family celebrations and meetings with friends
The first date should only be about the two of you, his or your family and friends have no business being there. To be critically eyed by family or friends is a real mood killer and only makes it more difficult for you to get to know each other better.

• Party nights in clubs and discos
Party excesses with lots of alcohol go down well with very few people. If you are both regular party people, there is nothing wrong with sharing this with each other, but it is better to wait until at least the second date. The same applies to places and events where boozing is inevitable: folk festivals or festivals are also a no-go for the first date.

• Concerts and cinema visits
This point is admittedly controversial, because concert and cinema visits do not provide a good opportunity to get to know each other better through conversation. On the other hand, they are

great for quieter people to get a feel for each other. So if you share the same taste in music or movies and are casual about it, such visits are not to be disregarded.

WHERE TO GO NOW FOR THE DATE?

You now know what makes a good dating location and which ones you should avoid at all costs. Of course, you should now also get a few concrete suggestions.

Culinary Dates
Eat out

• Italian: Going to the Italian restaurant is quite a classic. There's certainly something for everyone and it's a place you can't go wrong with.

• Sushi: For friends of Japanese cuisine, a sushi restaurant is ideal. The great thing about it is that you can share the small bites with each other.

• Tapas: A tapas bar is a place for socializing and good food. Here you can have a great time, share food and enjoy the casual atmosphere.

• Ice cream: If you want to meet on a warm day, there is hardly anything better to snack on a cool ice cream. Eating ice cream is a great way to combine it with other activities, such as a short tour of the city, as it can be bought and eaten along the way. Alternatively, you can sit down in an ice cream parlor and enjoy it there.

• Brunch: The middle ground between breakfast and lunch, a fabulous invention. If you have something planned for early in the day instead of the evening, a small brunch is a good way to eat together and get to know each other better. Brunch can also be a great way to start a slightly longer date.

Make your own food

• Cooking: Well, for this it is certainly necessary that you meet at one of you at home, but cooking together is still a good chance to create closeness and get to know each other a bit on the side. It's also a great second or third date.

• Barbecue: Especially in the warmer months, there's hardly anything better than sitting outside in the fresh air and eating freshly grilled food. If none of you has a grill, a disposable grill and an outdoor fireplace suitable for grilling will do.

• Picnic: Similar to a barbecue, you can sit out in the fresh air and eat the goodies you've brought along. Make arrangements beforehand so that you are well provided for. Take a blanket with you and then make yourself comfortable, but be careful: picnicking is more of a fair-weather activity and not the best choice in heavy rain or thunderstorms. Check the weather conditions before your date and have an alternative plan if necessary.

Going out for a drink, non-alcoholic

• Milk bar: Even if they have become rare, they offer delicious non-alcoholic drinks and food.

• Café: Another classic for the first date is a visit to a café. From hip and alternative to traditional, there is a wide variety of restaurants that offer you coffee and cake, other nibbles and, above all, a relaxed place to talk in the right atmosphere.

• Juice bar: A freshly prepared delicious juice is a great companion to a casual conversation and especially good for a little break before moving on. Together you can discover and taste extraordinary creations.

Going out for a drink, alcoholic

• Wine tasting: First a visit to an exciting exhibition and then a wine tasting - a dream for the culturally inclined among us. Tasting through different wines as a couple, enjoying them and casually chatting along the way sounds like a very romantic first date after all.

• Beer garden: For the more down-to-earth, a beer garden can offer a relaxed alternative. Enjoying the fresh air and a cool beer in the middle of the greenery, perhaps accompanied by delicious food or a small snack - it doesn't get much more relaxed and informal than that.

• Cocktail bar: The cocktail bar, on the other hand, can be a bit more stylish. It is usually the ambience and not the drinks that make the date a very special one.

• Christmas market: Although temporally in the year only limited possible, but if it offers the opportunity, certainly one of the most popular places for dates. Enjoy together the lovingly decorated stalls, the smell of roasted almonds and spices and of course a cup of strong, hot mulled wine.

Sport dates
Doing sports, with each other

• Jogging: A popular sport, especially for women, but it's even more fun for two on a date. So you can turn together quite relaxed a round through the park, while you improve your condition at the same time.

• Bike tour: Do you prefer to travel faster? A bike tour can be combined with a picnic outdoors or you can find an interesting place to visit. Even if you don't have a specific destination, it can be a lot of fun to simply ride your bike side by side as a couple.

• Dancing: A popular couple activity is to shake a leg together. So why not do it on a date with someone you're just getting to know? You can get a little closer and will definitely have fun, whether you are gifted dancers or not.

• Climbing: For the daring, rock climbing is a nice activity for a date. The possibilities are many and it will surely be a date that you will remember.

• Ice skating: Ice skating is a particularly romantic sport. To make the ice unsafe before the visit to the Christmas market or to seek some cooling in the ice rink in the summer - both are possible.

• Rowing: This sport requires good teamwork and coordination, but also strength. Relaxing a bit afterwards and enjoying the work-out you did together is a great way to end this date.

• Skiing: For the more extravagant date, a trip to the ski slopes is also possible. This does not necessarily have to go to the ski resort, but ski halls offer a good alternative to still have some fun in the snow.

• Bowling: Whether with or against each other does not play a big role here, because playing bowling can be a lot of fun. Not quite as strenuous, this activity is also suitable for sports fans.

• Frisbee: A sport that can be combined very well with other activities in the beautiful, fresh air. And you don't need more than a Frisbee disc, it can be that simple!

• Skateboarding or Longboarding: If you both or one of you enjoy skateboarding or longboarding, isn't this a great opportunity to get on the board together and practice some cool tricks or just relax and cruise around. It's worth giving it a try.

Doing sports, against each other

- Minigolf: Whether outdoor or special black light minigolf - here you can compete, but above all have fun and laugh a lot.
- Billiards: Also suitable for a relaxing afternoon or evening. The good thing is that many bars have pool tables. After a round you can sit down again comfortably and get to know each other better over a drink.
- Table tennis: Tables for table tennis can be found in many parks. So all you need are two bats and one or more balls. This sport is great for some exercise and fun in between.
- Tennis: If table tennis is not enough for you, you can also play tennis. Together you can have a good game and really work up a sweat.
- Badminton: If you play this sport seriously, it can be very fast. If you don't really want to go out on the field, you can find a green meadow in nice weather and play the ball to each other in a very relaxed way.
- Squash: Squash is a backstroke sport that requires either a special court or a simple wall, as well as a racket and a ball. It's a great opportunity to try something new.

• Fencing: Primarily a martial art, where you'll compete against each other as clear opponents. This experience will definitely give you something to talk about.

• Go-Kart: Something for those who like it fast. Here you can prove your driving skills and compete against each other.

• Boule: Boule, like boccia, is representative of all ball sports. What counts here is skill. In addition, this game offers the opportunity to entertain yourself a bit.

View sport

• Stadium: How about a visit to the stadium? If you're both sports fans, the stadium is a good place to share a fever and get a feel for each other.

• Pub: In addition to cigarettes, beer, cocktails and snacks, many pubs have TVs that you can use to watch a game. Alternatively, you can go straight to a sports bar, have a chat there and watch the sport on the side.

• Couch: You can relax on the couch at home. If you're both fans of computer games, you can watch e-sports or see what else the TV and Internet have to offer.

Dates in the fresh air
In the city

• Sightseeing: Sightseeing in a city you don't know allows you to discover exciting things together. Choose destinations that interest you in advance and enjoy your stay in these special places.

• Guided tours: A great way to get even more background information on sights is to book a guided city tour. This way you don't have to navigate yourself and have more time to absorb the exciting impressions around you.

• City park: In many cities there are very beautiful, spacious parks that invite you to a nice walk, a little picnic or duck watching. A visit to the park can be easily combined with other activities.

• Zoo: A visit to the zoo is even more exciting. There you can see native animal species up close and even feed and pet some of them. Watching cute baby goats together will surely bring you closer together.

• Amusement park: Action is the order of the day at the amusement park. You will certainly have fun and entertainment here. The visit is suitable if you plan a whole day together, because here can pass gladly times a few more hours.

• Flea market: There is a lot to see and talk about while strolling around. The flea market is a great way to get to know your date's interests and tastes.

In the country

• Hiking: A mix of light athletic activity and nature enjoyment. Many places offer beautiful hiking routes, from which you can choose one, or you can wander around spontaneously and find the paths that appeal to you the most. While hiking you can entertain yourself, but also stop and enjoy the surroundings.

• Boat ride: As far as moving around on the water, there are many options. You can take a short boat ride across a river and explore new places or rent a boat at a lake. Romantic moments are guaranteed here!

• Kite flying: Windy weather is called for here. When flying kites you can be a child again and have fun together.

• Mushroom picking: Autumn is a particularly good time for two people to go mushroom hunting in the forest. But other seasons also bring out one or the other type of mushroom. Fresh mushrooms can also be used in a joint cooking evening.

Cultural dates
Listen

• Comedy: Where better to laugh than at a comedy event? There will certainly not be many opportunities to have a quiet chat, but the fun factor is guaranteed.

• Cabaret: Cabaret offers similarly good entertainment. You'll have a great time here and will certainly have plenty to talk about afterwards.

• Poetry slam: Poetry slams are a suitable meeting place for friends of modern word art. At this event you can listen in pairs, think and have stimulating conversations afterwards.

• Reading: You are true bookworms, like the same authors or like to be sprinkled with words? Then a reading might be the right date idea for you.

• Concert: Enjoying an evening of loud music together is a beautiful experience. If more than one artist is performing, you will also have the opportunity to exchange ideas during the breaks and have a drink in a lively atmosphere.

• Club: There are also stylish clubs where binge drinking is not the main focus. Here you can dance, drink cocktails and really celebrate your get-together.

• Dance class: Shaking your hips together while dancing brings you closer not only physically, but also personally. With a little openness, even a complete beginner is sure to have fun and learn something new.

• Browse your vinyl collection: Do you or your date like to collect records, CDs or cassettes? Music can also be enjoyed and shared within the four walls.

View

• Museum: Exhibitions in museums provide an excellent basis for conversation. Whether it's ancient works of art, giant skeletons of already extinct animals, or technology, there's a museum for just about every topic.

• Theaters: These are places where many things come together: art, music, drama and usually also a long tradition. So they're perfect for anyone who enjoys cultural activities and wants to get away from it all for a while.

• Cinema: When many people think of a date, they immediately think of a visit to the cinema. Even if the conditions for getting to know each other in conversation aren't the best, at least you can sit close to each other and share a bucket of popcorn - it's romantic, too.

Do it yourself

• Photography: Whether it's taking pictures of each other or picking out exciting photo subjects, if you go on a photo tour together, you'll definitely have something to capture this special gathering in pictures forever.

• Drawing class: Sitting down by yourself with a sketchpad and pencil can be insanely relaxing. Going to a drawing class as a date is definitely an experience that is special.

• Karaoke: No one needs a top-notch singing voice to have fun at karaoke, because that's what matters in the end. Not taking yourself too seriously goes down well with everyone and guarantees you a good time in any case.

• Jamsession: Do you both play any instrument or sing? Making music together connects in a very special way. Either create your own piece or play songs by your favorite artists.

• Campfire music: You've had a picnic or barbecue outside, it's now dark and time for some music. It doesn't have to be the classic acoustic guitar. Listening to a small music box is also an option if you don't have anything else at hand.

THE RIGHT OUTFIT FOR THE DATE

The question of all questions - What should I wear? Admittedly, it is an absolute cliché that a woman needs hours to find the right clothes before a meeting. But as we all know, clothes make the man, or at least have a not inconsiderable influence on the first impression we make. Even small details reveal more about us than we think, and can even lead to the other person either finding us immediately likeable or the exact opposite is the case. You can't please everyone, but it doesn't hurt to think a little about what to wear on a date.

There can be no universal formula for the perfect outfit, but I'm sure everyone will agree on one thing: the clothes should match your personal style and you should feel comfortable in them. You now know that authenticity is enormously important when getting to know someone, and if you force yourself into a skimpy dress and high heels when you're more the type for casual jeans and sneakers, you won't be able to give yourself as you really are. So, refrain from any disguises, no matter how promising they are touted by many a guidebook. Stay true to yourself and your style, because then you will radiate true self-confidence and that will be more attractive than any piece of clothing. But, if dresses, skirts, high heels and lots of jewelry are part of your everyday wardrobe anyway, don't hesitate and wear what you feel attractive and comfortable in. Your outfit also doesn't have to be either hyper-feminine or very casual and sporty, because with clothes like a pair of trousers and a chic blouse, most people can certainly feel comfortable.

Furthermore, you should of course adjust your outfit to the type of date. In the previous chapter, you were presented with numerous ideas and I certainly don't have to tell you that a cocktail dress and high heels are not the most suitable choice for a very sporty meeting - clearly. Such meetings are more about activity and togetherness, but you should still appear well-groomed. A natural look is also more attractive than having to constantly check whether your outfit, hair and makeup are still in place.

If a visit to the opera is in the offing, on the other hand, a somewhat more upscale dress code is called for here than, for example, in the ice cream parlor, that should also be obvious. Don't think too much about the date and what the man you're going to meet might like, but instead think about where you're going, dress accordingly, so that you feel beautiful yourself, but also confident in your skin. This way you are on the safe side and avoid the unpleasant feeling of being over- or underdressed.

Also, before each date, stay positive and assume that you will not see the person for the last time. Thus, you will definitely have the opportunity to show your richness of facets during the next meetings.

GREET YOUR DATE

The day and the time have come, your first date is coming up. You might ask yourself how you should greet the man with whom you have been in contact for quite a while now. Of course, a greeting always depends on the situation, and your age and the way you were brought up and where you grew up may also play a role. Below you will find some options, which are sometimes more and sometimes less suitable, but in many cases it arises anyway in a spontaneous way, as it fits best at the moment.

• A handshake

The traditional and classic greeting is a simple but firm handshake. Among younger generations, this form of greeting is becoming increasingly rare - logical, because it doesn't have a particularly warm effect. It also maintains a certain distance and seems rather formal. You should at least make sure to smile friendly and look your date in the eye, because the right facial expressions can make a big difference.

• A simple "Hello

A rather cool way to greet someone, and therefore not particularly recommended. Breaking the ice after such a start could become a difficult task.

• A hug

A short hug immediately breaks the barrier between you and makes you not feel like you are on a forced meeting with a distant acquaintance. A short but determined hug with a friendly facial expression is already enough here.

- Kiss left, kiss right

As an alternative to hugging, you can give each other a peck on the left and right cheek. For some, however, this greeting may seem unfamiliar and overpowering, so be careful if you are not sure. Most of the time, your gut will tell you what is appropriate and what is not.

After the greeting is over, it is important to find a suitable transition into a conversation. If your date doesn't ask you first, ask him how he is or if he found his way here. A conversation will develop from this as if by itself.

YOUR TOPICS OF CONVERSA-TION

If you are one of those cautious people who plan things, meetings or even conversations in advance, this will certainly also apply to your date. With all the excitement, however, it can be really difficult to think clearly and to think about what you want to talk about at all. After all, you certainly already know one or two details about the person and do not want to ask the same questions over and over again. Especially in a personal conversation, however, you can learn to understand your counterpart even better, because you exchange subconscious signals that are completely lost in the chat. As far as the content of your conversation is concerned, you should first get a few suggestions.

• Everyday life

Such a simple topic, but also one that everyone can contribute to. Tell each other funny stories that have happened to you or your friends. Not only will you learn about each other's daily lives, but you'll also learn about the people you hang out with. Don't just talk about yourself, ask questions and let your date have their say too. If you're the quiet type, try to overcome your taciturnity a bit so that the conversation doesn't become one-sided.

• Profession, study, etc.

What happens to you in your job, studies or apprenticeship is also an everyday topic that you can talk about on a date. After all, each of you probably spends not a little time every day on professional activities or the like. However, don't talk exclusively about this, but this point can be a good start, especially at the beginning, to get to know the other person a little better. For example, talk about your professional goals, what you might want to change, what you've been doing well lately, or what funny things sometimes happen. Ask your counterpart, for example, why he likes his job or why maybe not and what he dreams of instead. In this way, you create a transition to other topics of conversation.

• News

A less personal topic, but still a good stimulus for conversation, is current affairs, which include political decisions, for example. You may learn less directly about him as a person, but you will know afterwards roughly what makes him tick on other levels and what values he represents. For many couples, a certain basic consensus on political and social matters is very important, and it certainly takes tolerance and openness not to be immediately put off by opposing views. As long as you are both interested in discussing such issues, keep it to the more positive matters and don't dwell too much on the bad, because after all, you want to associate your meeting together with something beautiful.

• Travel

A neutral topic that is good for understanding y-our date a little better is travel. Talk about where you've been, what places you'd like to go, and what your dream vacation would be. Also, ask what other plans your date has or what his worst trip so far was and why. This will almost certainly result in one or the other beautiful or entertaining story.

• Hobbies

A very obvious topic, but it should still be mentio-ned again. Even if you already know what your counterpart likes to do in his spare time, it can't hurt to go into more detail in a personal conversa-tion. Ask him why he likes to do exactly what he calls his hobby. If he answers openly and honestly, you'll be much closer to learning more about who he really is. For many, hobbies like sports, art, or music are not just hobbies, but central to their li-ves and something that seems to have a higher purpose behind it. Depending on what your counterpart is ultimately interested in, it is exciting to listen more closely and ask questions. In the same way, of course, you can tell about yourself if he shows interest or asks questions.

• Books and movies

The worlds created in books and movies provide yet another unique basis for conversation. If you're both interested in books and movies or one of each, talk about what you're currently reading or have recently read and what movies you like. If it turns out that you have similar tastes in movies, suggest that you go to the movies together so that you have an incentive for a second meeting.

• Visions and dreams

It gets a bit more profound with conversation topics like visions and dreams. This is less suitable as an introduction to a conversation. Tell about your own wishes for the future and when you would like to achieve them, but also ask your conversation partner about them. Clear plans for the future can also help you determine whether or not the two of you are a good match for something long-term. Above all, you will find out what moves your date and what his deepest dreams and desires are - and that already reveals a lot about a personality.

• Future plans

Somewhat less onerous, but no less important, is the topic of future plans. This refers to concrete plans such as career plans and wishes for children. But a general forecast of where you see yourself in five or ten years is also very exciting to share. Here, too, you can find out whether you agree on certain important points or whether you differ completely.

• Philosophize

The longer your date has lasted, the more profound the topics usually become. So it sometimes happens of its own accord that you philosophize about topics that may not necessarily occupy you consistently in everyday life. A date is a great opportunity to exchange ideas in this regard. What is truth, love, the meaning of life? Can there be free will and would we all be happier if we were stinking rich? What is happiness? Long, enriching conversations can develop from questions like these as food for thought.

• Commonalities

People with whom we have something in common are often immediately more likeable. So pay attention during the conversation to what your counterpart tells you, because there could be something that interests you as well or that you also like to do. Afterwards, you can deepen the conversation and perhaps find one or the other idea for a next meeting.

WHAT YOU SHOULD NOT TALK ABOUT

Not every topic of conversation is suitable for a first date. Some things create a bad mood for both of you or simply put you in a bad light and that's exactly what you want to avoid. In this short section, here are the absolute no-go's when it comes to topics of conversation.

• Problems, money and worries

You should avoid depressing topics that worry and upset you. Say that you do not want to talk about it at the first meeting, should you be asked about it.

• Your ex-partners

No matter what you could tell about your ex, don't do it on the first date. Talking negatively about ex-partners doesn't exactly give the other person the impression of a good character and also the fear that the same thing could happen to them if the thing with you should be through at some point. But talking too positively about an ex-partner doesn't go down well either, as it could then seem like you're not over said person yet. You see - it's best not to bring up this topic at all.

• Religion and politics

Even though current events can provide a good basis for conversation, it's not always easy to maintain a positive atmosphere among each other when it comes to topics like religion and politics. If you feel that the conversation is drifting too far into the negative here, steer it back to another lighthearted topic.

• Sex and tenderness

Overly spicy questions and topics should not necessarily be part of your first date, unless you are both just looking for a casual relationship like a Friendship Plus. Talking about such topics can otherwise convey the wrong intentions.

PAUSES IN CONVERSATION ON THE FIRST DATE

Many dread them - the awkward pauses in conversation that can slowly build up on a date and then become more awkward over time. But why do we perceive pauses as awkward? It's an embarrassing situation for most people, although the problem lies more in our feelings and how we deal with it. Probably everyone has experienced it at least once: A conversation that was going great until just now stops abruptly, we suddenly can't think of what else we could say because our head now doesn't allow us to think clearly either, and that unpleasant, embarrassing feeling spreads. A rather inappropriate question as a stopgap will not save the conversation either, at least at this moment. So what can you do instead? It can help to think about the topic a little more, since it is certainly a true horror scenario for many on a first date.

The cause of this phenomenon is that there is a great deal of uncertainty at a first meeting. The insecurity is not directly related to possible disinterest on the part of the other person or even to the fear of rejection, but rather the lack of familiarity is the cause behind it. If one thinks about it, speech pauses and even longer silences are not at all embarrassing. After all, being together with family, friends or other very familiar people would be very uncomfortable as soon as silence comes up, but in the environment we know, this is usually not the case. Now, on the other hand, when we meet someone for the first time in real life, we tend to immediately question and interpret the meaning of silence. It is difficult for us to perceive the pause in conversation as simply pleasant, because this familiarity is missing, but on a date it is very good to give the person you are talking to and yourself a short break to pause.

A good trick to soothe this unpleasant feeling is to address the pause in the conversation specifically, but to remain humorous and self-deprecating. Openness breaks the ice, and your conversation partner will certainly be relieved that it's not just him. Turning such situations into a conversation immediately creates a looser atmosphere and will possibly provide new conversation material right away. If you don't let yourself get flustered, you'll come across as confident and humorous.

Reserved men were already discussed at the beginning of the book, and so it can also happen to you that a date in real life suddenly seems more shy than you would have thought. A conversation can therefore be a bit tough if the man you are meeting does not have a great need to communicate. You can draw such people out by asking the right questions. Surely you have some things in common, otherwise it would certainly not have come to your date. So be specific about these hobbies and interests, but avoid questions that can be answered with a simple "yes" or "no". So ask open-ended questions that provide plenty of conversation potential and content. However, you shouldn't pester your date with questions, because it shouldn't feel like an interrogation or job interview for him. Just sprinkle in a few of your own anecdotes and little stories here and there. It is possible that one or the other question will be put back to you, from which a good conversation can slowly but surely develop again.

However, avoid jumping from one topic to another at all costs, but instead go into depth and try to derive new questions from what has been said. A really interesting conversation is characterized by depth; there is no need to scratch the surface. So follow up so that what is said does not remain one-dimensional.

MIRRORING - A SECRET BODY LANGUAGE TRICK

Besides purely verbal communication, body language is also an incredibly powerful tool. Most of the time, our gestures and facial expressions are completely unconscious, which is why it can be so useful to analyze your dating partner's body language, as it can reveal more about them than what they say about themselves in terms of content. At the same time, however, you need to know that you can use your body language quite specifically to create a certain impression in your counterpart. This works not only on a date, but really everywhere. Do not underestimate the impact of your body language and learn now what exactly the trick of mirroring is all about, because it can help you to effortlessly gain a few more sympathy points.

Body language includes our gestures, facial expressions, posture, the way we move, and all the other things we can express nonverbally with our bodies. There are also the so-called micro-expressions, also called micromimicry, which refers to fleeting facial expressions. These are difficult to impossible to control. Our gestures, on the other hand, we can control and use to influence other people. This phenomenon is called mirroring. Did you know that over the years, married couples have become similar in their body language and automatically mirror each other? Even people who hold the same opinion usually adopt a similar body posture. Professionals can even manage to imitate the way their counterpart speaks, which makes them particularly easy to influence.

Numerous studies show that people who mirror their own body language are rated better and are perceived as more likeable. The only important thing here is that the mirroring does not become an imitation. If you are too tense and try to imitate even the smallest movement, this will quickly be noticed and achieve the opposite effect. So if your date takes a sip from his glass during a visit to the café or bar, take a moment before doing the same.

Apart from mirroring, there are of course other things you should consider with regard to your posture if you want to maximize your chances of success on a date. Eye contact is very important, because if we often look in another direction, it tends to suggest disinterest. It's perfectly normal to break eye contact every now and then before resuming it, because a constant stare doesn't always go down well either. With good eye contact and a slight smile, you are definitely on the right track.

Also, do not hold any objects directly in front of your body. This can be just a small coffee cup or a bag. Holding something close to your body can convey to the other person that we don't want to have anything to do with them, feel uncomfortable in their presence, or are very insecure.

If you are sitting across from each other at the meeting, make sure that your body, and especially your feet, are pointing in the direction of your date if you are sincerely interested in him. Eye contact has no effect if your body is sending the opposite message. It is similar with folded arms: Anyone sitting across from you like this comes across as dismissive. So keep your arms open, too; after all, open body language also shows openness to the other person. Don't constantly tug at your clothes and certainly don't constantly look down, because that also shows little enthusiasm.

As you can see, this topic is an incredibly broad field. Just be aware at your meeting that you can convey something specific with your body language and take advantage of its powerful effect with the help of mirroring!

WHO PAYS ON THE FIRST DATE?

From secret body language, let's move on to the more practical matters that you may encounter on a date. It's about the question of who picks up the bill when visiting a cafe, restaurant, bar, etc. In the past, this question was easy to answer and even today, some may still clearly answer, "The man, of course!". Nowadays, the matter has become a bit more complicated.

Why was it customary in the past that the man always paid? Let's keep in mind that until 1977, women were only allowed to work if it was compatible with their family and marital life. Until 1958, the husband could even terminate his wife's employment without being asked if he considered it to be detrimental to the marriage. Women's access to the labor market was thus made extremely difficult for a very long time, from which it followed that most of the money lay with the husband and he accordingly invited the wife to dinner. All this was not so long ago and has only slowly changed as a result of the emancipation of women, which of course also changes the question of who should pay at the first meeting.

Let's go through different scenarios. It is possible, for example, that the man tells you in advance that he wants to invite you. You, on the other hand, have the option to accept or decline this invitation, after all, there are women who may feel patronized or dependent if the man insists on picking up the tab. It is ultimately a decision that you should answer for yourself in a way that you feel comfortable with.

In movies, you often see the so-called "reach" in such situations on a date, the grab for the wallet with which the woman wants to signal that she is also willing to pay. Who finally picks up the bill is not so important, but what counts is that the other person feels appreciated. It usually happens quite spontaneously in this way, if it has not been agreed beforehand who invites whom and the waiter suddenly stands expectantly at your table.

This brings us to the next scenario, or rather the next tip. The easiest way is to decide in advance who will pay. So if you would like to take over the bill, tell him clearly that you would like to invite him and avoid misleading language. Of course, there is always the possibility of splitting the bill if nothing has been agreed upon beforehand. It's even better if the date goes so well that you want to see each other again, because then you can agree that one of you pays on this date and the other on the next.

Also worth mentioning at this point is a positive psychological effect that occurs when the bill is not shared, but only taken over by one person. This is called reciprocity, which means that the invited person feels the need to give something back. On the other hand, the person who invests something also feels more sympathy for the other person. Incidentally, this can also be immaterial things such as time or special effort and expense.

So you see that both inviting and being invited has its advantages. Ideally, you should simply consult with each other beforehand to avoid unpleasant situations.

SEX ON THE FIRST DATE?

Many experts agree: sex and other intimacies on a first date don't have to rule out a committed relationship. The most important thing is that you and your dating partner know what you both want and know your principles. If you rule out any intimate acts on a first date as a matter of principle, that's perfectly fine and otherwise it's totally fine too. So why is the topic still under discussion?

In a survey of a well-known online dating site, out of about 1600 singles, 23% of men and one-third of women said that sex steers them in the wrong direction on the first date. The fears are loss of interest and creating a bad impression. So it's not a few people who like to slow things down when dating, because the fact is, if you like each other, you'll still have plenty of time to get to know each other on an intimate level.

So why wait? Even if a good relationship is not impossible after early sexual contact, it is difficult for us not to reduce the other person then only to the sexual, whereby the honest interest in the person could fall by the wayside. It can be exciting to take your time, but most importantly, you probably won't miss the opportunity to talk about your intentions and expectations. What do you hope for from each other? Do you want a relationship that is short term, long term, or just fun? If you become intimate early on, communication may be lost because one or even both of you may assume that your relationship is now settled and that this is a relationship start. There is always the possibility that it remains a one-night stand.

The cliché of the "easy girl" is unfortunately still quite persistent, which is why many women shy away from getting involved in something, even if they actually want to. If a man loses interest in you because you had sex early on, that doesn't speak well for him. So listen to your gut, because if you're right for someone, the quality of the relationship won't suffer if you haven't waited long.

As with the question of the bill, it is very uncomplicated here if you simply clarify in advance what you expect and what is absolutely out of the question for you. If you are against any form of intimacy on a first date, make that clear to him. This will take some of the pressure off each other, since you know what you can and can't expect. But what if you haven't discussed it beforehand and he takes the date in a direction that doesn't suit you? If it gets too intimate for you, tell him clearly. Both parties have a clear obligation to respect each other's boundaries. If it ever happens that your date ignores your boundaries, feel compelled to end the date. Stay true to yourself and never be persuaded to do something you are not comfortable with.

HOW DO I INITIATE A SECOND DATE?

During your first date, you're blown away and already know for sure that you want to see him again. The only question is how you should go about it. If he also found the meeting pleasant, it shouldn't be a difficult task. But what is the best way to go about it?

Sometimes the opportunity arises during the first meeting to arrange a second one immediately. It doesn't matter who makes the suggestion. Does he talk to you about it and say he would like to see you again? Great, in this case the matter is easier than perhaps thought, because in fact men communicate basically very directly when they want to see you again. But the question for a second date does not always come from the man, so if you have the impression that he enjoyed the meeting as much as you did, you can of course take the step. Tell him, for example, how much you liked the meeting with him and from his reaction you can usually guess whether he feels the same way and whether he would like to see you again.

Alternatively, wait until after the date and text or call him instead. A simple text message usually proves to be a good choice, as you again give him the space and time to think about it and respond when it suits him. You can proceed as you would in a real meeting. So write that you enjoyed the date very much and wait for his reaction. Maybe he will take the initiative and ask you first, but if not, you should not miss the chance. He may just be insecure and not want to lose contact with you if it turns out that you don't want a second date. The gut feeling usually shows quite clearly whether a second date is possible or not.

WHAT IF HE DOESN'T WANT A SECOND DATE?

When men are not very interested in the woman during a date, they usually show it quite clearly. The good thing is, if you have a good gut feeling, it is rarely the case that it deceives you. But what do you do if you ask him for another date and he refuses? You should also be prepared for that.

If you spent a really nice date, you already had butterflies in your stomach and are already thinking about further dates with him, it is of course a pity to have to receive a rejection. The truth is: he is not interested. You should finish with it and move on. Trying to convince him anyway seems pretty desperate, doesn't go down well and simply doesn't work. But since you are both adults at the end of the day, you can still thank him for the good time and end the contact on good terms.

In some cases, dating can develop into good friendships, but this is only possible if there are no feelings involved, or at least if they have already faded. If you continue to be interested in a man, however, do not try to develop a friendship with him. This carries the risk of continuing to get your hopes up and being disappointed again. Be aware of what you are ready for and what you actually want, and act accordingly.

THE COMMUNICATION AFTER THE FIRST DATE

You've made it, your first date is over. You come home and the thoughts start to circle: "What happens now?". It's good to get some distance on this first, so you can better assess the situation. In fact, it is mainly the women who like to arm themselves and withdraw after a first date. Without overdoing it by signaling to him that you're no longer interested, this tactic isn't so bad, provided the man you're dealing with is into it. Men are not very reserved when they like a woman, and so it can happen that he contacts you the same evening. How it will ultimately go on with you, however, also depends very much on how your date went. So let's first go through various scenarios.

• Scenario 1: Your meeting went great
You definitely like each other and both obviously had fun on your date. The good thing is, you can hardly do anything wrong by simply listening to

your gut feeling. If you are on the same wavelength, you don't need a strategy to stay on the ball. You should definitely let your date know that you enjoyed it and would be happy to meet again. Pulling back a lot when you are actually sure that you like him is not the most appropriate thing to do.

However, you should avoid showering him with messages right away. Take things slowly and do not immediately talk about joint plans for the future and family planning, because otherwise there is a risk that he will feel put off by this behavior. Nevertheless, give him enough space for himself.

• 2nd scenario: the meeting was a failure
Not every date results in sympathy, and some dates can even turn into a real flop. In any case, you're sure that it won't be enough for a second meeting. How do you deal with such a situation? Be honest and respectful to your date and tell him that you are not interested, so you can both finish with it and go your own ways.

However, you should not give him false hope by saying that you can meet again sometime. Also, avoid abruptly breaking off contact with him and simply not contacting him again. That would be quite unfair and you wouldn't want the same thing to happen to you.

• Scenario 3: You are unsure of yourself

Also, not every date either goes great or turns into a flop. Sometimes you may have the feeling that you do not know how he felt about the meeting and whether it could become more. In this case, the first thing to do is to be calm and wait and see. It may take a while before you get the first spark, and you should definitely give him another chance. It is still too early to decide whether you are compatible or not, and it is also completely normal not to know right away what this is supposed to lead to between you.

In any case, you should not make a rash decision and write him off completely. After all, there is a possibility that you will have a few more wonderful meetings and that it will develop into something more.

As you can see, there's no great reason to panic after the first date. Most people tend to get really crazy, even though that's not justified. Think of a first date as a casual get-to-know-you session, because that's what it's for - to get a first impression of each other, casually. Even bad experiences are valuable here, because they let you know what you definitely don't want from a date and future partner, and they prepare you for the next opportunity.

Men flatter

Who doesn't like to be flattered? A sincere compliment goes down well with everyone and so of course men are also happy about some recognition, even if they may pretend not to be into compliments. The fact is, men don't get compliments often enough and by telling a man about his positive qualities, he will feel appreciated. So the next time someone compliments you, return the favor. The following points will tell you what men like to hear.

• Compliment him on his looks. Men are also happy to hear that they have beautiful eyes or that you think they look great. There will hardly be a man who will not feel flattered by this.

• Compliments aimed at the man's strength are also well received. This works especially well if you already know each other better or are in a relationship. For example, if he carries the heavy shopping, acknowledge this with a nice saying.

• A compliment that appeals to a man's protective instinct is to tell him that you feel safe with him. This also gives him a sense of strength and being needed, it's an ego boost for him in a way.

• Tell him that he is smart. Compliments on intelligence are also well received, if the situation allows.

• Acknowledge him in public as well. Small compliments, which you announce in front of other people, give him confirmation and a good feeling.

• Use superlative compliments à la "You are the best". This will make him feel like a true champion and very flattered.

He distances him-self

The following scenario: You have known a man for a short or long time, possibly you have already met or had several dates, so you are not (yet) in a relationship. Slowly and insidiously, you have the impression that he is distancing himself from you more and more, contacting you less often and, if at all, only answering briefly and succinctly. This can have many reasons and does not necessarily mean that he is no longer interested in you. Distancing is not a rare topic on the part of the man as well as on the part of the woman, which is why it is worth taking a closer look at it.

DISTANCE DOES NOT EQUAL DI-SINTEREST

Just because a man, with whom you were previously still in good contact, suddenly contacts you less often, does not necessarily mean that he loses interest in you. The mental merry-go-round that then starts has something to do with your perception and attitude. Yes, you read that right - so it doesn't make sense to get crazy about it. Many people know this fear that everything could be over again very soon, and maybe you have also had this nasty fear that someone is gradually losing interest because they contact you less often or even cancel meetings.

Of course, there can be numerous reasons why he distances himself. Stress at work, family circumstances, illness and so on and so forth. Even if these are all legitimate reasons for needing a little more time for oneself, in most cases the cause lies elsewhere. So, if he doesn't convincingly demonstrate on his own that it is external circumstances that are forcing him to distance himself, there is most likely something going on subconsciously. He may be put off by an old pattern he knows from a previous relationship, for example, that is happening to him now, so that he is unconsciously seeking to withdraw. It is also likely that he is still unsure of his feelings and therefore wants to gain some distance in order not to hurt you and himself with a hasty decision.

KEEP CALM

The best thing you can do now is to stay calm and by no means fall prey to madness. Sure, if you had a very nice, intense getting-to-know-you phase at the beginning, you're used to enjoying his attention. The brain produces more of the happiness hormone dopamine, which is known to us as the feeling of the infamous butterflies in the stomach. Now, if that man you fell head over heels in love with goes away, it feels like going cold turkey. That in turn means stress, and stress only makes you feel crazier. A vicious circle is created. Now you just can't overreact and keep asking him out or spamming him with messages. This is the last thing a person who is looking for some distance wants.

But how can you escape this horrible mental merry-go-round? Look at it this way - by paying less attention to each other for now, it also means you've gained time. Time for you. He, in turn, has enough time for himself and can focus on what's important to him right now. Now it's time with y-our friends, pay attention to what you need right now, and treat yourself to it.

It should also not degenerate into a fight between you. The one who keeps the other wai-ting the longest wins? Never. At the very least, such games aren't much fun. Of course you would like to know where you stand with him, that is completely understandable. But, by trying to force or fight for something, all the ease of getting to know each other is lost. While there's no guaran-tee that everything will work out the way you both want it to in the end, it's still better to stay calm instead of questioning every little thing.

All the negative feelings you experience when he supposedly acts different and more distant than usual are actually just a product of your own head cinema. The real reason why a previously good getting-to-know-you phase comes to nothing or even a relationship suddenly breaks up is very often great distrust in the partner or the person you are dating. Behind this is the fear of not being good enough, in whatever form. Conversely, the opposite of this mistrust and fear, that is, a healthy confidence in yourself, leads to a strengthening of this connection between you. With confidence in yourself and that everything will be fine, it is much more likely that everything will take a positive course.

This downward spiral and emotional roller coaster doesn't start when you think he's distancing himself, but much earlier. It's ultimately self-sabotage that you engage in when you're seriously interested in a man, since you've probably already had bad experiences in that direction. By interpreting something into every little detail that confirms your own fears, you save yourself from the next disappointment. The feeling of having found someone you are simply blown away by, but for whom you think you are not good enough, is simply too powerful. If such behavior patterns with exaggerated panic pushing sound familiar to you, you shouldn't just go on unreflectedly like this.

You have exactly two options. The first one is to react to his distancing in the usual way, because it confirms your own basic bad feeling towards y- ourself. By reacting reproachfully and with anger, you push him further away from you, because the certainty that he is really no longer interested is better to bear than the uncertainty. Waiting for the man of your dreams will never end this way, because the relationship will be sabotaged even before it can solidify.

The other, obviously better option is to get a grip on one's emotions, distance oneself from them and analyze what is really going on. In the case of a supposed distancing, there is often no se- rious cause for concern. You should internalize this thought and thus build more self-confidence. It is not easy, but by having your thoughts under control, you will be able to go step by step in the right direction.

The pattern is usually expressed in such a way that the affected women enjoy their meetings and contact very much, but when they do not see each other again for some time, they fall into fear and insecurity. They prevent themselves from really enjoying their own happiness. As mentioned earlier in the text, now is the time to listen to yourself and just enjoy everything. If everything else is going great and you just suspect that he is distancing himself emotionally, this assumption or rather fear is not justified. Instead, be happy that you have met someone who likes you and whom you also like, and look forward to what can still become between you.

Try to think very specifically about what your fears are in this context, and maybe even write them down. Are you afraid you'll never see him again? Or do you think he will soon break off contact with you? Is there perhaps another woman involved? Or maybe you fear that he just wants to keep you warm? Then think about how much these fears have to do with his true behavior and intentions. The bad thing about this head trip is that these fears feel very real. The worst-case scenario has practically already happened and you're just impatiently waiting for it to finally come true, but it pretty much won't. If you ever find yourself in this situation, you'll see that everything was ultimately much more harmless than you thought.

The good feeling you regain as soon as things go on with him as before may lull you into carelessness at first, but this merely puts the mistrust back into the background. You have to actively work to overcome it while it lasts, because otherwise it will return in a similar way every time and ruin your chances.

OVERCOME YOUR OLD PATTERNS

You can only overcome your old behavior patterns by consciously noticing and living through your feelings from the beginning. With time, you will be able to observe how your fears in the form of his behavior do not come true at all, and thus you will be able to build a trust in him and yourself. With this newfound trust, it will suddenly be perfectly okay to go down that uncertain path that once scared you. Overcoming this old behavior can become an insanely educational experience for you and strengthen your self-esteem on yet other levels, because you can apply your strengthened confidence to all other areas of your life.

GET HIM OUT OF HIS RETREAT

Still, the question is how you can lure a man back, because working on your own attitude is one thing, and not simply ignoring the problem is another. By doing the same thing as him, that is, taking a break first, you mirror his behavior. But it's understandable if you find it difficult to take this step, because there might still be the fear of losing him for good.

The unconscious withdrawal can, as already mentioned, be due to the fact that he felt restricted by too many feelings on your part. If you now give him less attention and contact him less often, he will certainly not forget you. It is only likely that he will turn away if you make it clear to him that you are not interested in him. Otherwise, there is no serious danger that you will be forgotten and never hear from him again.

You must understand that for men, only at the very beginning of your getting to know each other, a certain basic interest on your part plays a role. Thus, in phases of distance, the desire for a long-term relationship can strengthen, as your balancing relationship connects you closer. By the way, this does not only apply to the case that you are just getting to know each other, but can also be transferred to relationships that have already lasted longer.

A certain, very special female competence is required on the part of the woman: namely, the competence to recognize unloving behavior and to withdraw from this situation without reproaches or complaints and to concentrate on his own life. This is not to say that you should completely break off contact for a time, but a man wants to see that a woman is not emotionally dependent on him, but emotionally stable. Of course, unkindness and coldness will not do you any good and that is exactly what you need to realize. Temporary emotional coldness on his part, however, you must not automatically confuse with disinterest. This may all sound a bit paradoxical, but it is incredibly important that you listen to yourself in such a situation. What is important in your life right now? Don't make him responsible for your own happiness, because that is not only unattractive, but can massively prevent you from being happy in the first place.

Be sympathetic to your partner or the one you are dating, but still with a certain distance. This shows him that you are not satisfied with anything less than the best version of himself. Your behavior will show self-respect, which is really important for a healthy relationship. It's also about giving each other the freedom to take care of their own lives, which is the exact opposite of constriction. It is this constricting feeling that often drives men into distancing themselves. With a decisive but lovingly conveyed short or even longer break, the relationship can usually be revived.

HOW TO MAKE HIM MISS YOU

Many men share the need to withdraw from a relationship or a getting-to-know-you phase every now and then. You now know that distance from each other does not have to immediately mean a bad sign for your being together and your future, but can restore a healthy balance. How you can skillfully make him miss you again in these phases, you will now learn in a few points.

1. Don't wait for him - do your own thing.

Many women make the mistake of giving their partner or the person they are dating his space, but show that they will wait for him. "Just get back to me when you're ready," they might tell him, or, "I'll be there when you need me again." But you shouldn't let him have full control. Show him that he can't disappear from your life and then re-enter as he happens to be funny. Signal to him, when the time comes, that while you are happy to let him into your life, it is not possible on his command.

2. Don't just react to him - act yourself.

Waiting means reacting to his behavior. But instead of letting him do everything to you, you should meet him at eye level and act yourself. This also clearly means that you have to distance yourself from time to time as soon as you notice that he is making little effort. It is an unconscious test of the man to see how far he can go with you. If you put up with his coldness for too long, he will see it as a lack of self-respect and will be able to have less respect for you. Know your limits and take the reins yourself.

3. Don't be on call all the time - focus on your own life.
He comes back to you after a while and asks for a meeting? You should not give in that easily. In a way, you should make do, but don't misunderstand. It's not so much about artificially shorting the supply when there's demand, but rather focusing more on your own needs.

4. Don't coldly dismiss him - put him off in a loving way.
Even if his behavior may hurt you a little at first, do not be offended or even insulting, and do not be reproachful. Do not start complicated discussions, because they will not help you at that moment. Instead, you should be sympathetic. This attitude on your part will convince him of your strength and make him long for you again after some time.

5. Don't overwhelm him with attempts to contact you - get back to him when it's important.

It should be clear by now that it's never good to bombard someone with text messages. Don't write to him just to say hello or about trivial things, but only get in touch during your break when it's really important or when you have some peace in your own life and have time for him again. The same applies to phone calls, because here the rule is: less is more.

Commitment Anxiety

Nowadays, it is becoming more and more common for people to be afraid of making a firm commitment to another person. The fact that there seems to be a general trend toward this could be related to the way the topic of dating is approached. Online dating in particular means that everyone with Internet access theoretically has the opportunity to reach out to a large number of other people. "There could be someone among them who is even better suited to me than she or he is," is usually the internalized belief. Yes, the possibilities have become more diverse, but that is not only a blessing, but also a curse. Young people in particular find it increasingly difficult to commit to one person, because the man or woman of their dreams could still be out there.

In truth, the search for the perfect relationship and the perfect partner doesn't make us any happier because we simply feel like we never arrive. But we also don't want to miss out on anything, because no one can give us back our lifetime. The great fear of emotional closeness, of something that is final and binding, the fear of letting someone very close into one's life, causes a great many people to freeze once they have found someone with whom things are going well, or else those with commitment anxiety seek out relationships that are doomed to fail from the start, sabotaging the event unconsciously, that is, even before it really begins. The individual reasons for commitment anxiety can be different and because it is such a hot topic, it is worthwhile to take a look at it. That is what this chapter is about.

THE CONTRAST BETWEEN CLOSENESS AND DISTANCE

Everyone needs and desires closeness, and this naturally includes those with commitment anxiety. Those affected get into a dilemma because many of them enter into relationships or even marry, but suffer because they can't let their partner get too close or open up to them. In order not to disappoint their partner or a potential candidate, or in order not to make themselves dependent, they then keep their distance. But the constant conflict between the need for closeness and self-determination remains, which can become a major hurdle in relationships at times.

THE CAUSES OF ATTACHMENT ANXIETY

Two causes in particular are responsible for many people suffering from commitment anxiety. These include:

1. Traumatic experiences

Very formative, painful experiences in connection with previous love relationships can cause a person to develop attachment anxiety. But the cause is not only buried in love relationships, because it is especially the early childhood experiences that significantly shape our attachment behavior. The loss of a person can also have such a negative impact on future relationships.

2. The attachment relationship in the first years of life

Attachment anxiety is a protective strategy that the psyche builds up over time to prevent further painful experiences. If a child experiences little affection from its first attachment figures, usually its own parents, especially in the first three years of its life, this can have a massive impact on its later attachment behavior. In this case, the child develops negative beliefs and internalizes them on a subconscious level, which can also influence life as an adult if these beliefs are not dissolved. Sentences like these can be "I am not good enough" or "I can only rely on myself". As a result, getting involved with a person is perceived as dangerous, more dangerous than the need for self-determination.

As you can see, the causes of attachment anxiety are often not superficial, but deeply rooted in the psyche of the person concerned. This knowledge will initially help you to better understand the phenomenon called attachment anxiety and to be able to deal with it.

TYPES OF ATTACHMENT ANXIETY

People with attachment anxiety can basically be divided into two categories. They are closely related to the beliefs one acquires as a child.

Protection strategy of autonomy and self-determination

Affected persons who learned as a child that they can only rely on themselves and may be hurt again as soon as they let someone get close to them belong to the avoidant type. The very thought of getting firmly involved with someone and thus putting their self-determination at risk seems so dangerous to the affected person that firm relationships are avoided from the outset. It is nevertheless possible that they want to date and get to know other people until it fails as soon as the other person considers a relationship. As a result, a person with commitment anxiety usually quickly seeks escape.

Protection strategy of clinging and holding on
It is somewhat different with those who have internalized in childhood that they can only earn love and do not get it unconditionally. It may sound unexpected, but these people tend to cling very tightly to their relationship at times, just to avoid losing their partner. There is a tremendous fear of loss behind it, sometimes coupled with delusions of control, which, if nothing else, can lead to the person's partner eventually turning away. This means that those with attachment anxiety, who tend to use the protective strategy of clinging and holding on, enter into relationships, but then change over time.

HOW CAN YOU RECOGNIZE COM-MITMENT ANXIETY?

The symptoms of this anxiety manifest themselves in different forms. Men with commitment anxiety tend to behave a little differently than affected women, but basically, in many cases, the problem can be easily identified by a few signs. If you fear that you're dealing with a relationship phobic, keep your eyes open for the following symptoms.

• Break contact
As soon as things get serious between you, he seeks escape by unexpectedly breaking off contact with you. Especially when you have become very close emotionally or otherwise, this is seen as a last resort to maintain your own self-determination. This behavior is also known today as ghosting: the person who breaks off contact disappears from the other person's life like a ghost, and without regard for that person's feelings.

- Emotional coldness

Rejective behavior is also often exhibited when someone suffers from attachment anxiety. Rejective behavior is in contrast to emotional closeness and thus maintains distance from each other. It is supposed to help not to let the partner or another person get too close, but be careful: not every distancing must immediately be a sign of fear of a committed relationship.

- Retreat

Physical distance can also be a sign. Men then often throw themselves into their hobbies, work or avoid physical proximity to the partner. The physical distance makes it easier to distance oneself further in order to continue to protect one's own autonomy.

- Lack of sense of responsibility

Obligations and commitments are avoided by the person concerned. In a relationship, this may manifest itself in the man leaving without telling, or neglecting and avoiding the things for which he has responsibility.

• Indecision

People with commitment anxiety find it difficult to make decisions concerning their own relationship. A sign may also be that the person is extremely insecure about a budding relationship and does not know what he or she wants. Constant on-off relationships also indicate problems with attachment.

• Refusal to plan a common future

People in a committed relationship usually intend to plan a future together. However, someone who is very insecure due to their fears will avoid this as much as possible and react evasively when joint ventures or plans that lie in the future are brought up.

• Surprising separations

Those who get involved in a relationship despite commitment anxiety often break up completely immediately. At the beginning of the relationship, everything may still seem fine, but as time goes on, the attachment fears have an increasingly strong effect, so that the person concerned ends the relationship in order not to be hurt by the other person later on.

• Poor choice of partner

A somewhat hidden sign lies in the choice of partners that people with commitment anxiety make. Thus, some of them choose partners with whom a relationship is doomed to fail from the start.

DIFFERENT BEHAVIOR IN MEN AND WOMEN

Since attachment anxiety manifests itself early in childhood, men as well as women can be equally affected by it. The causes of this and the effects on the lives of these people is therefore very complex and individually different. However, it is possible to identify certain commonalities between the sexes, because the phenomenon manifests itself somewhat differently in women than in men.

Men often fear losing their autonomy and being restricted in the togetherness of a committed relationship. They don't want to miss out on anything and keep other options open, so they often want to stick with open relationship models.

They then believe that they simply haven't found their dream woman yet, but don't realize that the cause of their dissatisfaction lies elsewhere. Since they want to avoid being hurt (again), men prefer to stay on their own and take responsibility only for themselves.

For women, on the other hand, it is often a high level of expectation that prevents them from finding their love happiness in a serious relationship. With the increasing desire for self-determination in society, which is important and justified, the need for self-determination in a relationship is also growing. While there is also a desire for a committed relationship, women unconsciously make choices that make such a thing impossible, for example, by being very picky or looking for partners who are unattainable and with whom a serious relationship is difficult.

HOW CAN YOU DEAL WITH HIS FEAR?

If the signs indicate that your (potential) partner is afraid of a firm commitment, this is certainly difficult to digest at first. This is a complex issue that will not be resolved overnight. But commitment anxiety can be overcome step by step, and by showing understanding and support, you will succeed even better.

In order to overcome such a complex problem, the insight that this problem exists and the desire to overcome it must come from the person concerned himself. It can be exhausting for you if your counterpart is not aware of his fears, but it is useful to involve yourself in the process of overcoming in order to help a little. You should act with understanding and accept his fear of commitment at first and help him to perceive and accept the problem.

The next thing to do is to find out the causes of the anxiety. Since, as already mentioned, these lie buried deep in the psyche, triggered by experiences in one's own childhood, it can make a lot of sense to seek professional help. Depending on the severity after which the relationship is affected by the anxiety, it makes more or less sense to seek a place in therapy, so it does not have to be absolutely necessary. Especially since you need a lot of patience for this and it can cost some overcoming to confide in a complete stranger. Your possible or already steady partner can also look for the reasons on his own or you can make it a joint task. He should consider what his negative beliefs are and how they relate to his childhood experiences and to your relationship.

This self-knowledge should help him change his behavior in situations where attachment anxiety is having its effect. It is a process that you can guide him through, not by trying to convince him of something through argument, but by reinforcing positive experiences. Through affirmation, recognition, and love, you can help him gain an improved sense of self-worth so that he can build greater confidence in himself and, ultimately, in you.

Note that this process can take years. So a lot of patience and a positive mindset is needed to get through this together. Also, there is a danger of getting into a vicious cycle if you think you can rescue him from his anxiety. By trying too frantically to reach him, you may cause him to withdraw further and break up abruptly if you make further advances. However, if he admits to himself that he has a problem, the chances of improvement are good. So be sure that this awareness is present in him before you take further steps.

ARE YOU READY FOR A RELATIONSHIP?

Perhaps you have asked yourself whether you are ready for a relationship at all. You may have even recognized some behaviors and thought patterns and are now wondering if you are not also affected by unexpected fears. But there's no need to panic, because self-knowledge is the first step to improvement, as the saying goes.

So, if you suspect that you have a problem with your relationship ability based on the signs listed before or also on experiences from previous relationships, the prerequisite to overcome it is the will to achieve it. Next, you should think about possible causes. An alternative is a therapy that is more emotion-focused. The aim is to become more aware of your emotions and to find out which behaviors result from them and how you can replace them with better behaviors. This form of therapy is said to be very promising and can ideally support you in achieving your goals.

You can also try to manage anxiety gradually without therapeutic care. If you have a partner, this is the ideal opportunity to involve them in this process. In the previous section, you learned what you can do if you want to help someone overcome anxiety, and your partner can do the same for you. However, even if you are currently single, it is possible to work on this problem. You can work on exploring the causes of your negative beliefs and replacing them with positive ones. The main thing here is to strengthen your self-esteem and confidence in yourself and other people. Then, the next time you find yourself in a situation where you start dating someone, you can react immediately when old patterns of behavior arise in you.

As soon as things get more serious between you with a man, feel free to bring up the subject. He will appreciate your openness and will certainly want to help you if he is seriously interested in you. It is important to find a balance between commitment and autonomy, that is, the ability to open up to the other person and to want to be emotionally close to him, but also to give each other space to enjoy and shape their own lives. Everyone is capable of relationships and is able to find happiness if he or she just takes the necessary steps.

Create emotional closeness and bonding

Imagine you are in the following situation: You have met your Prince Charming and after some time things start to get more serious between you. But something is missing and there is still no real emotional bond between you to move from this transitional phase into a committed relationship. You will surely wonder what you can do to help a little bit or to increase his serious interest in you in the first place. We would like to approach all these topics in this chapter.

CREATE THE RIGHT ATTRACTION

There is no universal recipe for triggering the feeling of attraction in a man, because our perception of attractiveness is a complex construct. What we perceive as attractive is influenced by factors such as our own desires, our subjective perception of beauty, but also by where and how we grew up.

Optical stimuli often play a central role in first impressions, because the first thing you perceive about someone when you see them in real life is their appearance. Every person has his or her own ideal of beauty, and it's usually the people who roughly correspond to this ideal who catch your eye. A man who totally blows you away visually may therefore be completely uninteresting to another woman, and the same applies vice versa.

Besides looks, life experience can also be very attractive. This is especially true for people who are looking for a long-term relationship, because a lot of experience, also with other relationships, usually goes hand in hand with emotional maturity and a certain self-confidence. Your own desires also play a role here, of course. If your counterpart is looking for something long-term, a woman who knows what she wants in her life will be very attractive to him.

The security that a potential partner can offer one is also not to be neglected. This includes conveying loyalty, emotional security and support, as well as protection and care.

In addition, body language plays a major role when it comes to attraction. The topic of mirroring with regard to nonverbal communication has already been addressed here and it not only shows superficially who is attracted to whom, but also reveals who really suits you on a profound level. Unconsciously synchronously executed movement sequences show who is on the same wavelength with whom.

These features make men's hearts beat faster
Men are attracted to women by different characteristics than women are to men - this is perfectly logical. In the development of attraction, unconsciously perceived sexual attractants, so-called

pheromones, come into play. They indicate to what extent someone is a good match for us on a biological level and whether healthy offspring would be produced with said person, regardless of whether we have a desire to have children or not. Men therefore generally attach importance to stimuli that indicate a high estrogen level in the woman.

1. Female figure

Most men prefer a feminine figure with curves, the so-called hourglass figure. Individual preferences can vary greatly, but the ratio of the hips to the waist is particularly decisive. A relatively narrow waist with slightly wider hips looks particularly feminine and attractive. A female figure looks particularly exciting when it is wrapped in red clothing. It is believed that the color red is associated with more sexual readiness and also represents a signal color in nature.

2. Child scheme

A high forehead, big eyes and a narrow chin - this is basically understood by the childish pattern. It triggers the protective instinct in men, making women with these features particularly attractive to them. A higher voice is also perceived as attractive, whereas a deeper voice can usually be accompanied by an equally powerful effect.

3. Friendly demeanor
A friendly, open-minded smile is sometimes all you need to instantly increase your attraction to a man. It shows openness and encourages him to approach you.

LET HIM HELP YOU

Men like to be able to feel like heroes for a change. But what does a woman need a man for these days? Since emancipation, women have become independent of men not only financially but also in other ways. But men's need to be needed is lost with it. This is not to say that women should become dependent again, that would be quite nonsense. Instead, you can show a man with small gestures that you gladly accept his help and thus make him feel like a hero.

For centuries, the man has played the role of provider: he ensures that the family is fed, has a roof over its head and protects it from possible dangers. At least, that was certainly still the case with our grandparents. In the course of the 20th century, this understanding of the role has gradually changed and the motto is: Self is the woman! Women can provide for themselves, maintain their own dwellings with manual skills and master their lives wonderfully alone as singles. But this primal instinct of men to still be the provider and protector remains largely untouched by this. It is possible that this will continue to change over time due to social change, but something like human instincts cannot be unlearned even in hundreds or even thousands of years. The desire to play the hero is so deeply ingrained in a man's disposition that it will not disappear so easily, even though external circumstances provide no valid reason for it.

Men like to take care of a woman because it provides them with some validation. You are doing both of you a favor by letting him help you more often, and this can also be integrated wonderfully into everyday life. He offers to drive you somewhere or pick you up? Or perhaps he would like to help you with a move and with the assembly of furniture? Feel free to accept these offers, even if you know you'd be great on your own. It's not about having to constantly demonstrate that you as a woman are independent and can manage everything on your own, but it's more of a give and take. Surely you can help him just as much with certain matters. Helping each other out creates a stronger bond between the two of you, and by gladly accepting his help, you also make him feel good. Now that's a win-win situation!

To flatter him even more, feel free to compliment him so that he feels appreciated. Words like "You're so strong" or "I couldn't have done it without you" sound like music to his ears.

GIVE UP YOUR LEADERSHIP FOR A CHANGE

When it comes to leadership in a (budding) relationship, it is similar to the topic of "accepting or giving help": It has become quite complicated nowadays. Just a few decades ago, it was crystal clear who was entitled to the role of leadership in a relationship, namely the man. This has changed over time, at least in our Western world, there is no longer a clear division of roles and the outdated understanding of what actually constitutes a woman or a man has been questioned and partly thrown overboard. This development was important, but at the same time it caused more and more uncertainty about what is still considered "appropriate" in the context of a relationship between a man and a woman. Is a man allowed to take the lead in a relationship or is this model outdated? Does he thereby belittle the woman? Or asked the other way around: Is a woman allowed to hand over her leadership to the man or does she thereby submit to archaic clichés?

Generally speaking, one could say that a man who has a healthy self-worth and does not suffer from commitment anxiety and thus wants to avoid his responsibilities, likes to take charge in a relationship. Similar to being protective and caring, being able to responsibly take the lead on certain relationship matters gives them a sense of validation. Many men want to do something good for their partners and at the same time, they enjoy the confidence that the woman gives them as a result. By handing over the reins from time to time and letting yourself be surprised, you also show strength. Giving up the lead also means giving up control, which in turn shows that you have a healthy self-confidence, in contrast to a control freak who constantly has to determine everything himself. After all, you don't have to fight frantically against old role stereotypes just because you think it's time to give them up. Instead, there should be a healthy balance - the art of remaining at eye level despite everything.

AWAKEN THE HUNTING INSTINCT IN HIM

You already got to know the hunting instinct at the beginning of the book. Admittedly, not every man is into eternal games consisting of an alternation of disinterest and attention. Openness and honesty is a good approach to any phase of getting to know each other. But awakening the male hunting instinct in your counterpart can not hurt to give the whole thing a little more pepper. Before we go into more detail later in the book, I'm going to give you three concrete tips to help you become even more attractive to a man!

1. Be authentic, have your own opinion and stand with both feet firmly in life. You should not

pretend and stand by your own principles. Don't let anyone belittle you! Be a bit cheeky sometimes. A self-confident but friendly demeanor is very attractive to men.

2. Don't always be available for him. You should have your own hobbies and pursuits to signal to him that you won't jump at it if he wants to meet up with you. Arming yourself - you've probably heard or read about this before. However, don't overdo it or he might misinterpret your absence as disinterest. No matter what relationship you have with someone, the important thing is to live your own life on the side and focus on things that are close to **your** heart.

3. It follows that you should not shower a man with love and compliments. With some people, this degenerates into love bombing, a pretty nasty manipulation ploy. In any case, lavishly giving attention is an absolute no-go. Compliments are okay, but in moderation. If you really shower him, you're more likely to chase him away instead of him wanting to "chase" you.

4. Don't be afraid to meet other men besides him. As long as you are still in the non-binding first getting-to-know phase, it can't hurt to keep other

options open for you. This way, a man knows that you are also desired by others and thus he has competition. What awakens the hunting instinct more than knowing that you have to fight for what you want? Of course, you should not overdo it, because with 20 different candidates, you also lose the overview at some point and you get to know each one only very superficially.

If you follow these tips and he falls for you, it is equally important to give yourself to him afterwards. Reward his efforts by giving him your attention. If he hasn't turned away from you after a few weeks, it usually means that he is really interested in you.

PAY ATTENTION TO HIM

Despite all the games and back and forth, you must not forget to pay attention to a man of your desire. Paying attention to him does not mean that you have to overwhelm him with meaningless text messages. It also doesn't mean that you have to cling to him like a limpet that follows him wherever he goes and wants to read his every wish from his eyes. Too much attachment before you're even a couple could make him turn away from you as soon as possible, because it's just too much of a good thing for him.

Paying attention to a man means that you should be attentive to him. When we ourselves are very busy with a certain problem, we tend to talk about it all the time and not notice the other person. Listen to him when he tells you how he is feeling, and you will show your appreciation for him. Paying attention to him can also mean that you remember small details about him to please him with a surprise. It doesn't have to be anything big, because it's the little things that often carry a lot of meaning. For example, you find out during one of your meetings that he likes a special sweet very much or that he likes to drink a special wine. Remember these things and bring them to the next meeting or have them ready when he comes to visit you.

But the gift of attention should by no means be limited to material attentions. It is much more important, for example, that you give him your time, because this also shows respect for his person. Devoting your own time is one of the most valuable gifts you can give, because no one can ever return this lifetime to you. Of course, you also need to pay attention to your own life, especially if you are both very busy anyway, because during these periods there is no point in chasing after him. However, by regularly spending some of your precious time with him every now and then, you are signaling to him that he is important to you.

Paying attention to someone means that for a certain period of time you fully focus your attention on that one person. This is good and necessary for the emergence of a stronger connection between you and it will build an irresistible attraction. Ask him specifically about his thoughts and feelings and respond to them. In this way, you can also make him open up more emotionally, if he is one of those men who have difficulties with this. It is necessary to find the golden mean between giving space and giving attention, because it will be able to give you a harmonious relationship.

Treating each other with respect is enormously important, and yet many people just accept this without really thinking about it. What does it mean to treat another with respect? And when have you yourself perhaps unintentionally behaved disrespectfully towards someone? It is similar to paying attention: If you show respect to someone voluntarily, it is more likely that the other person will want to behave the same way towards you. Respectful behavior is not only a sign of a healthy self-image, but also a prerequisite for harmonious cooperation.

The word respect is used quite often and in different contexts in our everyday speech. When someone says "I have respect for dogs" it usually means "I am a little afraid of them and don't want to get too close to them". Respecting someone or an achievement, however, can also be an expression of high regard. "Respect!" is how we then congratulate someone we admire for their achievement. Respect can also be related to tolerance and acceptance, for example, when we don't necessarily approve of someone's decision, but still want to tolerate it. In summary, respect stands for values such as appreciation, politeness, esteem, acceptance, but also reverence. They are an important part of our social coexistence and our individual interpersonal relationships with strangers, acquaintances, friends or even partners.

So what does it mean to be respectful to a potential partner? The likelihood of problems arising from a lack of respect right at the beginning of your acquaintance is relatively low. Lack of respect is primarily something that only creeps up after a longer period of time, when partners take their mutual existence for granted and have discovered that he or she will not leave them, even if they humiliate their partner. But it's still possible for someone to treat you disrespectfully right at the beginning of getting to know you, or to quietly hint through their behavior that they themselves are constantly looking down on other people. You should listen to your gut feeling if you notice that there is something fishy going on and he is not showing you enough appreciation on his part. However, the first thing we want to talk about here is how you can show respectful behavior yourself, because it's no use just blaming the other person. So let's take a look at a few points, what you should pay attention to and what you should and should not do.

• Don't blame him.

For example, if he cancels a meeting or does not contact you for some time, this does not necessarily have to be a bad sign. Therefore, do not reproach him, because these are usually based on assumptions that stem from your own interpretation and emotions. Instead of reacting in an offended manner, you should communicate with him in a friendly manner and clarify matters in a mature way.

• Do not look for the blame only on him.

Some self-reflection is needed here. When something goes wrong and doesn't go as planned, there is rarely a single person involved. What might you have contributed? Show understanding and pause before you start blaming.

• Treat others with respect as well.

Surely you have also noticed people who treat others completely disrespectfully. Especially those who perform some kind of service for others, such as waiters in a restaurant, you should be friendly and well-meaning. You should also pay attention to how your dating partner treats strangers, but by not freaking out yourself over every little thing, you show that you are patient and would be a pleasant partner.

• Refrain from sudden breaks in contact.
Ghosting as well as benching are common behaviors that mean breaking off contact immediately and literally leaving the other person sitting and waiting. This behavior is absolutely disrespectful and should be avoided if you don't want to be remembered negatively. "Do unto others as you would have them do unto you" is an appropriate saying to internalize here. The same applies, of course, if you ever want to cancel a date or want to communicate that you are no longer interested in a man. Make sure you use as few hurtful words as possible and end things the way you would want him to end them.

• Respect his limits, wishes and needs.

By asking him about these things, you show him that you are not acting selfishly, but perceive him with his needs just as much and want to respond to them. Even if he wants to take it a little slower, you should respect this and not insist on clearly defining the relationship between you in the shortest possible time.

• Don't get insulting.

Especially in longer partnerships, it can happen with some that mutual respect is lost, which can express itself in insulting the partner. Words are not just words, but show very clearly what you think of the other person and how you feel about him. Insulting words have no place in respectful interaction with each other, even if it comes to an argument.

• Speak your praises.

Sometimes all we need to feel a little valued is a little praise. You can praise him for his accomplishments, but even better is when you express appreciation for his personal qualities.

• Stick to your promises.

Showing up on time for a date may seem like a small gesture, but it also shows a lot of respect. It shows that you know how valuable the other person's time is. In other matters, too, you should not make empty promises and then not keep them, because sticking to your own statements shows reliability and trustworthiness.

• Show gratitude.

Simply saying "thank you" more often shows that you don't take the other person for granted and are grateful that you get to spend your time with them.

BE OPEN AND READY FOR NEW THINGS

It's a great feeling to get someone excited about something and then be able to share it with that person. People who are open and curious have a very attractive and positive aura anyway, which tempts you to enjoy being around them. So if you sometimes feel that you are still closed to many things, this is the opportunity to change that.

A good way to practice more openness and willingness for new things is to look into the interests and hobbies of your dating partner. This way, you'll get to know him much better, since his interests are certainly an important part of his life. You may even discover a new passion for yourself, even if you do go your separate ways again. Moreover, you will create something that will connect you and give you more reasons to spend more time together.

The hobbies of the partner and especially those of the man are unfortunately often seen as a threat to the relationship. "You never have time for me" women then often complain about their partner. It is important to give him space and not to react with resistance when he wants to spend time on his interests. It is even better if you show understanding and interest, even if it is perhaps about something you admittedly have no idea about or with which you associate something you don't like. Once you deal with it, you will have a completely different view of it and pretty sure you will be able to take advantage of it for yourself. Moreover, women who show openness and willingness are irresistible and attractive to men.

Re-establish emotional closeness in a relationship

You have now received enough tips on the subject of getting to know men and how to deal with each other properly during the dating phase. But what about when you're already in the middle of a relationship? It's not as if everything has long since been settled and peace, joy, pancakes. It can happen that two people in a relationship slowly drift apart and lose the emotional connection to each other, which of course affects the relationship quality. I would like to give you a few tips to bring you and your partner closer together again.

• Brain research agrees that hormones have a massive influence on our sense of connection. During the infatuation phase, the happiness hormone dopamine predominates in our bodies, literally sending us into a kind of frenzy. We can't get enough of the other person and want to spend as much time as possible with them. Over time, this feeling gradually subsides, but that doesn't mean we become indifferent to our partner. On the contrary - the body then produces more of the bonding hormone oxytocin, which makes us feel close to the other person. We produce the hormone oxytocin primarily when we are physically close to each other, i.e. when we hug, cuddle, kiss or have sex. Instead of avoiding each other in times of crisis, it is therefore advisable to consciously seek physical contact with your partner.

• Open up your worlds of thoughts and feelings to each other. Relationship problems often arise when people stop talking and listening to each other. However, almost all problems can be solved with the right communication. So ask your partner specifically about his or her desires and thoughts and don't just listen, but respond to them and take up the topic again later. A close exchange will bring you closer together again and help you figure out how you want to shape your future together. What are his wishes and dreams and what are yours? Only when you talk about them, you will be able to consider how you will manage to bring them into fruition. Moreover, you can better interpret your partner's current mood if you know what is going on inside him at the moment. On the other hand, you should also tell your partner if something is bothering you and affecting your relationship.

• Learn to accept each other without compromise. Expressing criticism is important, and avoiding an argument will not lead to a good relationship in the long run if you just bottle up your problems. However, make sure you don't make your criticism sound reproachful. So use "I" messages, because you are not accusing him, you are just expressing how a statement or behavior of his came across to you. Then he also has the opportunity to correct this assumption without feeling attacked. Also, use more praise instead of reproachful-sounding phrases.

• Be aware that your partner is not a natural part of your everyday life. He certainly does a lot for you and you do a lot for him, even if it's mostly just little things. Express your gratitude because, after all, you are doing all this voluntarily and not because you are in a relationship of convenience.

• Admit your weaknesses and quirks. Nobody is perfect and you love your partner with all his weaknesses and he loves you in return. Instead of blaming him or her in an argument, you should admit to yourself that you are not flawless either and that you don't always act or react the right way. It can bring two people much closer if they know each other's fears and anxieties, because that gives a lot of insight into things that would otherwise go completely unnoticed. It is also interesting to do some self-reflection together and analyze what the problem is. Is perhaps fear of commitment the culprit? Admittedly, it's not easy to have such conversations, but you can only find solutions by also talking about the negative things.

• Spend more "quality time" together. After a while, a routine may develop between you, and you may find yourselves spending the evening together on the couch without a word and without really noticing each other. Think about how it was at the beginning of your relationship. You certainly had exciting activities and were naturally very interested in each other and exactly this dynamic is slowly lost over time. If you do more together and face challenges again, it will also bring you to a new level emotionally, because together as a team you are much stronger than alone. Romantic dates can also rekindle the fire between you and the feeling of closeness. So consciously take this time for each other and plan these meetings carefully.

PROXIMITY AND DISTANCE IN RELATIONSHIPS

The closeness-and-distance issue doesn't stop at getting to know each other, but can also play a major role in the midst of a relationship. Especially when the initial infatuation slowly subsides, it turns out that both partners have a different need for closeness and distance from each other. This then often looks like that one person of both still gives a lot of attention, seeks the closeness of the partner and would prefer to spend as much time together as possible. For the other person, on the other hand, this becomes too much at some point, so that they may even have doubts about the relationship and withdraw for the time being. The partner, in turn, then feels offended, unloved and fears that it could soon be the end of the relationship.

You may have also read or heard a few times that it is the men who withdraw after some time and then usually rush into work or a hobby. As a partner, it can then seem as if the hobby or whatever it is that he is busy with, is much more important than the relationship and questions the meaning of the same, if you hardly spend any time together. But the other way around, there can also be women who withdraw, to which the man in turn reacts without understanding.

The problem with this is that you can easily be blinded by your own emotions and not be able to look at what is actually happening soberly. If you ever find yourself in situations where you think to yourself "He never has time for me!" or "He doesn't give me any space anymore," you certainly have a conflict regarding your different needs for closeness or distance from your partner. Try to look at everything related to this in a non-judgmental way. You now take the standpoint of a neutral outsider and look at your relationship. What do you see? You may see that your partner canceled your date in favor of meeting his friends because it is important to be in contact with people other than your partner. Only with outside input will your relationship remain exciting and alive, and his behavior doesn't mean he no longer enjoys his time with you. You may also see that your self-determination is not in danger, if you ever had that feeling, just because you are engaging with your partner. He is not forcing himself on you because he wants to smother you with his love, but simply because his behavior feels right to him and he has this same need to be close to you.

But that's not the end of it, because you can only be happy with each other when your needs differ if you talk about them and negotiate them as partners. Surely you've heard that it's important for a relationship to compromise sometimes, and I think that's important at this point to find your individual balance. This includes being clear about what you want and how much closeness and distance in the relationship is okay for both of you. Especially in stressful times when one partner is very challenged by work, exams, or other important matters, it can make sense to compromise here and say that you will each focus on your own lives for a short time. This is not to say that you must or should forgo contact during this time, but it should not feel forced. The important thing is that you remain sympathetic to each other and support each other in what you are doing, even if it is only with words.

Emotional distance can also develop between a couple if a quarrel has preceded it or if there are repeated small arguments that you could have spared yourselves. To avoid becoming even more emotionally distant from each other, you should not react defensively by withdrawing and ignoring each other, but rather tackle the cause of the dispute head-on and resolve it with clarity. Continuous, open and honest communication between two partners is practically half the battle of a happy relationship.

EXPLORES THE CAUSES

The best way to solve problems is to know exactly what is wrong. So if you are both unhappy with the current situation between you, try to explore the causes. Why aren't you as emotionally close as you once were? Are there obvious reasons like a fight or that you've been less physically close lately? Sometimes the causes are hidden and less obvious, which makes it easy to blame each other. You should avoid this and instead think about what the reason could be.

This is also a good opportunity to reflect on ourselves, because often the causes lie at least in part within ourselves and not directly in the interpersonal. For example, fear of loss or jealousy can cause one to grow emotionally distant if these things remain unspoken and unthematized. Feeling emotionally distant may be a temporary feeling, but if you seriously fear that things will go downhill with you over time because of it, you should urgently seek a frank conversation. It is recommended that both of you have had a chance to think about yourselves and the relationship beforehand. Depending on the outcome you come to, maybe even one of the tips mentioned above can help.

DO YOU REALLY FIT TOGETHER?

A question that sooner or later, whether during the process of getting to know each other or later in the relationship, everyone will ask themselves at some point: "Is this partner right for me and do we really fit together?" Even though there may be many construction sites in a relationship, you are certainly very attached to your partner and would not leave him or her overnight because you suddenly have the impression that it is not right after all. When we fall in love, we tend to overlook qualities that bother us, and this takes revenge later, as soon as you take off your rose-colored glasses. Is that a reason to just throw away the relationship? Not in most cases. Because there is no such thing as **the** perfect relationship or **the** perfect partner; instead, you learn to somehow come to terms with a suitable partner. That's why there can't be a perfect relationship formula either, because every person brings individual challenges and needs that you have to adjust to.

If the feeling of emotional closeness is lost once or temporarily, it is easy to question the relationship because it is hard to see at first glance whether it is a fundamental problem that is keeping you from a happy future together or whether it can be resolved relatively easily with a willingness to compromise. It's also not so important that you share every interest or hold the same views on everything. What matters is that you can understand each other through open communication, that you respect each other, share common goals, and hold similar values. If your relationship is still fairly fresh, you can get to know each other better by asking questions in this regard and find out if you are a good match. You can also write down arguments for and against, but this is something that ideally happens as you get to know each other. If you both feel like you fit together at the core, it's definitely worth strengthening your emotional connection if it ever weakens.

THE FIVE LANGUAGES OF LOVE - WHICH ONE DO YOU SPEAK?

Love knows no language - or does it? There are actually five different ways in which people express and feel love. The topic was coined by Gary Chapman with his book "Five Languages of Love". It can therefore be good to know your own love language and that of your partner, because it will help you to understand each other better and also give you a better understanding of issues such as closeness and distance. Which love language do you speak, which one does your partner speak?

1. Recognition - words of praise and affirmation

People who primarily receive love and communicate themselves in this language are happy to receive verbal or written encouragement. An "I love you" or a message with a compliment that comes from the heart is gladly heard and seen here. By expressing your affection in writing or speaking, the person speaking this language feels especially valued and loved.

Here's what you can do:

• Leave little notes, notes and send messages. Communicate your affection verbally, but also listen actively.

2. Togetherness - quality time together

If you speak this language, you want to spend as much time as possible with your partner. It's about giving each other undivided attention, having deep conversations, using your free time together wisely, and being fully present. The feeling of being listened to and being able to fully focus on each other without interruption conveys true love. Here's what you can do:

• Plan trips together or even a whole weekend trip with special moments.

3. Support - helpfulness in the name of love

Actions speak louder than words. People who show and perceive love through support want to make life easier for their partner. This can be small everyday tasks that are taken off the partner's hands when he or she has had a busy day. It's about showing love and not just expressing it verbally.

Here's what you can do:

• Saying "I'd be happy to help you with ..." more often or helping around the house and making the other person's daily life easier works wonders.

4. Gifts - attentions that come from the heart
Small attentions that you have thought about represent love in a visual way. They are tangible and can have great meaning and high symbolic value. By giving something, you show your appreciation in a thoughtful way and, when you receive a gift in return, you can express your gratitude for it. Here's what you can do:
• Think carefully about small, personal gifts and be grateful in return for what you receive.

5. Tenderness - physical touch and intimacy
Love can also be communicated in a very simple way, namely through touch. This can include exchanging intimacies such as kissing, holding hands, having sex, or simply cuddling and hugging each other. For those whose primary language of love is tenderness, physical contact represents an intimate emotional connection whose roots can go back to childhood, as parents also

convey their love through physical contact, especially to the still very young child.

Here's what you can do:

• Show and return physical affection, as it will further strengthen your sense of connection.

Did you recognize yourself in one or more of the points? What about your partner? Do you speak the same or different languages? Knowing the languages in which you show and receive love will help you understand each other better and work on your cohesion.

EMOTIONAL DUSTING

Contrary to many assumptions, the feeling of love is not indestructible and stable, but actually quite fragile. In order for this feeling and an emotional bond between two partners to develop and be maintained, it requires some care that we have to invest. Nurturing includes being open and honest with each other, as well as regularly sharing one's emotions, desires and needs. This all seems to sound self-evident, but in real life we can see that many people do not seek open exchange, but do not communicate certain feelings and thoughts to their partner. They remain unexpressed and unexpressed feelings and thoughts then accumulate like dust in our own homes if we do not take care of and clean them. It is even impossible to be well-meaning and to feel love towards our partner if we carry negative feelings inside ourselves instead. This makes sense from an evolutionary-biological point of view, but nowadays this mechanism gets in our way rather than helping us. The unexpressed emotions mask our feeling of love, so it's important to make order with them regularly.

This is where the so-called emotional dusting comes into play, because just as we clean our apartment so that it doesn't get dusty, we should also free ourselves from emotions that lie like a thick layer of dust over our relationships. Perhaps you have already felt the effect, whether in a love relationship or with other people - expressing your feelings is incredibly liberating and will immediately have a positive effect on your relationship.

It is fundamentally about working through and clarifying conflicts through open communication. In this way you heal your emotional injuries, become stronger together and also strengthen your connection. It is advisable to carry out this procedure regularly, preferably as a fixed part of your weekly routine. In this way, you can ensure that even small things that you might not otherwise discuss are addressed and resolved right away, because it's the small things that get to us when they add up over time and remain unexpressed.

Here, caution must be exercised in the case of false striving for harmony. Some people live in the belief that a relationship is happy and harmonious when you have no conflicts and keep quiet and avoid all negative emotions. This assumption is far from correct and counterproductive if you are striving for true harmony. Part of harmonious togetherness is being aware of conflicts and also dealing with them, but of course remaining respectful of the other person, since both parties should ultimately have a serious interest in getting negative feelings out of the way and strengthening their bond. Especially if you are already in a long-term relationship or are striving for one, you must not fall into the mistaken belief that harmony and harmony can flourish through suppressed arguments, because what actually happens is that the feeling of love and closeness between you will slowly but surely gather dust and at some point will no longer be noticeable.

Accordingly, it is recommended to integrate this routine into your relationship, at best, immediately. If you are motivated, you will quickly get used to it and find that it is a good way to restore emotional closeness. Even in the case of already dusty relationships, a real revival takes place. Try it out!

Dealing with narcissists

The term narcissism or narcissist is used quite often in our everyday language. By this we usually mean a person who is self-absorbed and puts himself above other people. So when we call someone a narcissist, it has a clear negative meaning, but the issue is not so superficial and easily clarified. Not every self-absorbed person is automatically a narcissist and we should be careful not to use this term inflationarily, but on the other hand, it is important to recognize real narcissism and to know how to deal with it then.

WHAT IS NARCISSISM?

To understand how to deal with a narcissist, you must first know what is behind it. Narcissism can occur as a characteristic of a personality, but also in a pathological form. One then speaks of the so-called narcissistic personality disorder, in contrast to the narcissistic personality style, which is less pronounced and not pathological. The probability that you will meet a man who is pathologically narcissistic is quite low. About one percent of the population is affected, and most of those are men. On the other hand, it is more likely that you will meet a man who has certain narcissistic characteristics, that is, who has a narcissistic personality style. Therefore, in this chapter we will focus on the personality style so that you can learn to recognize it and deal with it.

People with a narcissistic personality crave recognition and admiration. They usually do not handle criticism well and instead blame others, towards whom they often behave in a condescending manner. Since they also find it difficult to empathize with other people, it can be very challenging to deal with them.

Originally, the term narcissism comes from Greek mythology. One myth says that a young man named Narcissus fell in love with his own reflection and rejected all others. Even today, therefore, narcissism still stands for egotism, self-aggrandizement and exaggerated self-love, which is said to be increasingly common in our society as time goes on. No wonder - social media is teeming with selfies and unrealistic self-promotion that doesn't necessarily have a strong sense of self behind it. Narcissism is thus becoming an issue again and again, and relationships in particular are affected by it, although the actual pathological personality disorder has not yet been researched all that well.

Narcissism as a trait of a basically healthy person does not only have negative sides either. For example, such people are usually very ambitious and successful, and many of them are also in leadership positions.

CHARACTERISTICS OF A NARCIS-
SISTIC PERSONALITY

There is a whole range of behaviors that narcissists exhibit, but not every trait is present in every narcissist. Behavior can even change situationally, and just when you think you have this person figured out, they suddenly do something surprising. The traits can also vary in frequency and strength. With the following list, you have an initial guide to help you recognize narcissistic behavior.

• They leave a good first impression. As a rule, the first encounter with a narcissistic person is remembered positively because of his or her special appearance.

• Narcissists are very outgoing and communicative. They manage with ease to get into a conversation with other people and carry them away with their way of talking.

• They are very popular and have a downright attractive effect on many people. Narcissistic people enjoy the admiration and attention they receive and know how to win others over.

• They attach great importance to their status and are not afraid to brag about it. Narcissists also like to talk very openly about their wealth and other successes or achievements.

• Narcissists cannot admit to weaknesses and try to hide them. If something fails, they look for the blame with their fellow men.

• They cannot deal with criticism because it is seen as an unjustified, personal attack. Narcissists feel offended by it and hurt in their self-image.

• They seek the recognition of others. External confirmation and praise gives them the motivation to be ambitious.

• Narcissists surround themselves only with people by whom they are not criticized. This prevents them from being offended and also secures the recognition of those who admire the narcissist.

• To many other people, they behave condescendingly. By belittling others, they usually feel better about themselves.

• Narcissists cannot forgive other people. Once offended, the narcissist is unlikely to forgive it easily. Often they are then out for revenge.

• There is often great envy in them, because narcissistic people cannot bear to see that someone has more or something better than they do.

- They cannot empathize with the feelings of their fellow human beings. They thus lack empathy, which makes dealing with them a challenge.

- Narcissists are not good listeners, because they are first and foremost interested in talking for themselves and gaining approval for it. They are only interested in the opinions of others when it comes to recognition for the narcissist.

- They interfere in the affairs of others and pretend to have a say, if not a right of co-determination. In doing so, they often overstep the boundaries of their fellow human beings.

- Narcissistic people are very good at faking feelings. By using this deception in a purposefully manipulative way, they can get what they want.

- Apologies are difficult for them. Admitting guilt for something is unthinkable for most narcissists. For this reason, they assign the blame to everyone else.

- They talk others into feeling guilty in order to make them feel insecure. In this way, narcissists strengthen their own point of view.

- Narcissists often reach leadership positions. Since they are usually very ambitious people and attach importance to a respected status, they succeed in advancement. In such positions they can exercise power and the higher up they are, the more unhindered they are in doing so.

• They like to set rules and regulations. When everything goes their way, it gives them a sense of control.

• Narcissists join exclusive groups to set themselves apart from others. This makes them feel confirmed in their uniqueness and specialness.

That was quite a lot of identifying characteristics. You could also describe a narcissist with a few adjectives such as egotistical, boastful or stuck-up, but also intelligent, charming and strong-willed. Not every characteristic of a typical narcissist has to be extremely negative, because there can also be positive side effects. Furthermore, in no case does each of these characteristics have to be represented to be able to speak of a narcissistic person. Someone who fulfills the listed points for the most part and thus affects his environment has a narcissistic personality disorder for sure. However, this can only be diagnosed with certainty by a therapist, but most who present to a therapist come because of other complaints. Thus, the actual percentage of narcissists in the population can only be estimated.

Moreover, the characteristics do not have to appear immediately or in the same strength. It is possible that you get to know a narcissist, but at first only perceive his charming side, while possible manipulative, power-seeking characteristics remain hidden in the dark for the time being. Moreover, in a healthy person with narcissistic traits, a few of these characteristics may appear, but then they are not very pronounced.

From what one learns about the behavior and mindset of narcissists, one might think that they have high self-esteem, but in most cases the exact opposite is true. This can be seen, for example, in the fact that they are quick to feel offended by criticism and need to belittle others in order to feel better about themselves. Also, seeking affirmation and recognition on the outside indicate that there is nothing of this to be found within themselves. So there is no question of true self-love, even though their outward behavior initially conveys something to the contrary.

RELATIONSHIPS WITH NARCISSISTS

A partnership with a narcissist can be difficult, since he is primarily preoccupied with himself and cannot empathize with his partner. The relationship with such a person, who never sees the blame on himself and always wants to be right, is not possible at eye level at all, but can work for a while under certain circumstances. Knowing about such traits or even a narcissistic personality disorder, however, can help you recognize a narcissist and deal with the situation accordingly.

With regard to relationships, a distinction is made between overt and covert narcissism. In the case of overt narcissism, the partner impresses with his charm and self-conviction before or at the beginning of the relationship. Over time, the narcissist's character traits come to light, making the partnership more difficult and belittling the affected partner. The partner's function here is primarily to offer the narcissist confirmation and admiration and not to talk back. In the case of covert narcissism, the negative character traits are, as the name suggests, less obvious. The relationship problems are characterized mainly by envy and offendedness.

Narcissists who want to maintain their high-status self-image usually seek partners who voluntarily subordinate themselves to them and put their own needs on the back burner in favor of the narcissistic partner. Both extremes are individuals who have low self-esteem. The narcissistic partner, however, seeks validation in the recognition and admiration of the other, and that person, in turn, sees his or her purpose in relinquishing leadership and purpose and is content to be subordinate. So it is a harmonious, if not exactly healthy, relationship that can exist as long as the submissive partner does not rise up against the controlling behavior of the narcissist. A narcissist is unlikely to tolerate this contradiction, which puts the relationship in jeopardy unless both people recognize the problem and deal with it appropriately.

THE RIGHT WAY TO DEAL WITH NARCISSISM IN A PARTNERSHIP

As you can see, the topic of narcissism in connection with relationships is a delicate matter. It is important for the affected narcissist to seek professional help in the form of therapy or counseling. But it is also advisable for the partner to seek help elsewhere, since the partner of a narcissist suffers particularly. It is even better if the matter is tackled together, i.e. if both of you take part in couples therapy, because the chances of success are much higher.

In addition to targeted therapy, there are also some tips that will help you deal with a narcissistic partner.

• Keep your space.

It is important that you give yourself your own freedom in the relationship so that you can fully develop yourself. You should separate yourself and pursue your own positive thoughts, relax and allow yourself the time to form your own opinion.

• Know your own value.

Narcissists tend to put down those around them in favor of their own self-esteem and use the validation they get from them as fuel. But don't let them belittle you; look at your life and remember all that you have already accomplished on your own. Your self-worth depends on no one else but yourself. If your partner does not appreciate certain of your abilities, it is his loss, not yours.

• Don't make an enemy of your partner.

With all the frustration you might encounter in a relationship with a narcissist, you should not declare war on your partner. He, too, carries a previously unresolved conflict within himself that arose because he was probably deeply offended as a child. Narcissism is a compensation and protection strategy to avoid this offending in the future. So don't blame your partner, because he is only human and has to struggle with it just as you do.

• Don't take his ideas too seriously.

Narcissists can be capricious and jump from one plan to the next. In the end, only the fewest things are enforced. Keep in mind that narcissists will often contradict themselves and deny that they ever talked about anything after the plans came to nothing. Instead, wait patiently, because his constant changes of plans have nothing to do with you, but are simply part of his nature.

• Reduce your need for closeness.

A narcissist craves closeness especially when he needs something from you. Your needs are put on the back burner, but you shouldn't put up with that. Reduce your need to be close to him and don't be ready all the time when he needs you. Narcissists are very selfish in this regard because if you crave closeness but he is busy with something else, he will surely reject you.

• Give him confirmation.

Praise, affirmation and recognition from others is like a central driving force for narcissists. You are allowed to give your partner honest compliments and praise. Depriving him of this would not abruptly rid him of his narcissism anyway, but only make him very dissatisfied in the relationship. A healthy amount of praise and recognition, as you might wish for yourself, keeps the harmony going.

• Be the best version of yourself.

Narcissists want attractive and confident partners. While you should not do anything just to please your partner, by taking care of yourself, you are doing something good for yourself first and foremost. This will make your partner proud of you and like having you by their side. However, they do not like to be outdone by their partner.

• Pay attention to him.

You should listen to your partner carefully and show honest interest in him. Certainly, this is important to everyone in a relationship, whether they have narcissistic traits or not, but narcissists place a special emphasis on being noticed and paid attention to. However, don't overdo it and maintain a good balance so that he realizes that you are serious.

Some of the tips may seem contradictory, as they target exactly what a narcissist seeks and exploits. However, keep in mind that you should work with your partner, not against them. It is certainly a great challenge in everyday interactions, but if you react with extreme resistance, it usually does not end well. Of course, you should also feel into yourself and ask yourself if you can even lead a relationship with a narcissist or if it will drain y-our strength too much in the long run. Especially in very fresh relationships, such problems are quickly underestimated and this takes revenge o-ver time in the form of nasty repercussions. If you are sure that you could have a happy relationship - apart from his narcissism - you should plan a long-term goal. Therapy that involves both of you is certainly the best approach to solving the prob-lem. The tips mentioned above should help you on the way to your goal, which you and your partner should be able to achieve harmoniously.

The creeping beginning of a relationship

There is this strange phase between two people when they have been dating for some time and the question gradually arises "What's next?". Is it going to be a relationship? Does he even want a relationship? And am I sure that's what I really want? A lot of time can pass from the realization that there could be more between you to the official start of a relationship, but it doesn't have to. It is always advisable to take enough time, because if you are really interested in each other, you will not run away. However, if you are in this situation or you get into such a situation, it is normal to be a bit insecure and have a lot of questions. To give you a little more confidence, in this chapter you will learn about certain signs and get some food for thought on the topic of starting a relationship.

SIGNS THAT HE WANTS A RELATIONSHIP WITH YOU

1. He talks about a common future.
A fairly obvious and positive sign that he wants a relationship with you is that he talks to you about the future and plans together. He might also ask you what places you'd like to travel to or what else you'd like to experience, and may hint that he'd like to plan trips with you. He may even be talking about, or at least thinking about, what your daily life together might look like. Be attentive when he talks about such topics.

2. There is a balance between you.
If you want a relationship and he does as well, the attention and affection you give each other is

certainly in balance. You can tell this by the amount of time and effort he puts in, like you do, so he takes the time to respond to you at length to a message and doesn't constantly interrupt your phone calls prematurely. Of course, you both have your own lives to lead, appointments to keep, and everyday errands to run, but if he is genuinely interested, he will still always find time for you and not make you feel too emotionally invested.

3. He doesn't want to lose you.
The phrase "I don't want to lose you" can admittedly come from a man who likes me, but doesn't want a relationship with you and doesn't want to commit. However, someone who really wants to be with you will have already put a lot of energy into the connection between you emotionally and will not want to lose you because of that. This is one reason why men eventually want to be in a relationship, as they fear losing contact unless they clarify the relationship with you soon. Moreover, he will do a lot to maintain contact between you and make sure that you can see each other regularly.

4. He wishes for peace and togetherness.
If you notice that he obviously has no more desire for the fast-paced, he is surely looking for a permanent partnership. Fleeting contacts no longer give him satisfaction, but he longs for peace and quiet in order to be able to isolate himself somewhat from the rest. You can also see that this is his desire by the fact that he continues to distance himself from friends or acquaintances who continue to maintain this lifestyle.

5. He shows jealousy.
While pathological jealousy can be extremely damaging to a relationship, a healthy amount of it merely shows his interest in you. He would not like to lose you to another man and that is why he wants to have a relationship with you. However, be alert and cautious if his jealousy seems too exuberant.

6. He respects and values you.
Giving someone your precious time is not a given. If he wants a serious relationship with you, he is aware of that and appreciates and respects that you take time for him. When you meet, he is very

attentive and pays attention to you instead of just being on his cell phone or busy with other things.

7. Your conversations are more than just flirtations.
What he talks to you about says a lot about his intentions. If he shows serious efforts to get to know you better as a person, this is a good sign for a future together between you. Sure, flirting is part of it, but if it's just about sex between you and that's what comes out of your conversations or chats, there's not much relationship potential.

SIGNS THAT HE DOES NOT WANT A RELATIONSHIP

1. He cancels your meetings frequently.
It's perfectly okay to cancel a date sometimes, because sometimes important matters just get in the way, but if after a fairly intense dating phase you notice that he's canceling your meetings more and more often and doesn't want to initiate anything on his own, it looks rather bad for a relationship.

2. He has no time for you.

Here, too, the following applies: It's okay to be a bit busy and to have little time left for the other person. If this becomes a permanent state and he constantly comes up with excuses why he doesn't pay attention to you, it should make you think. If he was seriously interested in you, he would make time for you despite all that is going on in his life. Everything else only shows that you are not very important to him and that he cannot imagine a relationship.

3. He rarely gets in touch.

If he hardly invests any time and effort to keep in touch with you, the situation is clear: he doesn't want a relationship with you. Unless you are literally slaying him with messages or phone calls, it is very strange when a man with whom you had good contact some time ago suddenly takes forever to get back to you. Also, if he only replies very curtly and hardly asks about your well-being, he is not very interested.

4. He makes a disinterested impression.
If he seems rather uninvolved in your conversations and also shows no sincere interest in you as a person, he obviously has no interest in a relationship. He doesn't ask any questions and prefers to talk about himself, which keeps the conversation superficial and one-sided. If you notice such behavior, do not waste any more time with him.

5. It's all about sex.
Physical intimacy plays an important role before or at the beginning of a relationship, but if that's all you're focused on, there's little potential for a deep emotional connection. Pay attention to your gut feeling and don't ignore it if you notice that he hardly takes any time for you beyond sex.

6. He avoids the topic of conversation "relationship".
He constantly finds excuses or evasive maneuvers not to talk to you about how things should go on between you. He may still be unsure, but if there was at least a spark of serious interest in you, he would want to talk to you about it. If he clearly

signals that this topic is very stressful for him, you can forget about a serious relationship with him.

7. He doesn't introduce you to his environment.
During the getting-to-know-you phase, it can be difficult to introduce the other person to all your friends and family right away. But if he avoids your suggestions to get to know people from his immediate environment, this is not a good sign for you. If he can imagine a long-term relationship with you, sooner or later he will also want to introduce you to his friends or family.

8. He is still in a relationship or fresh out of one.
Contrary to any promises he may make to you, it is usually not a good sign if he is still in the middle of a relationship or has just had a breakup. He may just want to use you as a rebound or as a distraction to better deal with his predicament. However, there are cases where a happy relationship can still develop if he is sincere and honest with you. However, if something seems strange to you, don't get your hopes up too high.

MISTAKES YOU SHOULD AVOID AT THE BEGINNING

Whether you are about to start a relationship with someone or you are already in the middle of it - the beginning of a relationship says a lot about its future. If the situation is already very tense and complicated at the beginning, it is not yet automatically doomed to failure, but the cards are much worse than with a harmonious start to the relationship life together. So that you don't fall into any traps, I'll list some mistakes that you'd better avoid.

• Do not try to change it.

A popular mistake many women make is that they want to change their new partner. Not only does this not work in the vast majority of cases, it has a bad effect on your relationship. You have chosen this man as your partner, you are about to officially enter into a relationship with him, or maybe you already have, and you should stand by this decision accordingly. You should take him and accept him as he is. If in the course of your relationship something comes up that bothers you so much that you can't overlook it, you should raise the issue with him, but under no circumstances should you try to change a person on your own.

• Don't cling to him too much.
The fact that both partners' needs for closeness can differ drastically at the beginning of a fresh relationship has already been mentioned here. Accordingly, it is important for men to be able to continue their own lives alongside the relationship, and they expect the same behavior from their partner. Seeing each other more often for a while is still normal to a reasonable extent, but you must not give up your own social life for him. He cannot replace it for you, and once the intense feelings of infatuation begin to subside, you will find that you have become dependent on him for that. So avoid clinging to him too much and spending every free minute with him, even if it's hard at first.

• Arguing - but the right way.
Many people believe that avoiding a fight is the ideal way to live together in harmony, but the exact opposite is the case and when a fight does occur, the situation escalates. Arguing and expressing when you don't like something is part of a

healthy relationship, because you can't avoid conflicts forever. That's why you should learn to argue properly at the beginning or even before the relationship starts. If you have a problem with something between you, you should express what is bothering you in a matter-of-fact way instead of just keeping it quiet. It is always better than keeping your anger bottled up or being offended because of things you interpret yourself.

• Don't get ahead of yourself.
When you are in love, you like to already make plans for the future, imagine how you will move in together and maybe start a family someday. However, you should not be in too much of a hurry with such topics, because you still have enough time to get to know each other sufficiently. You should also take time to get to know your parents or friends. Don't be too quick about this and don't approach things with him until he is ready. At the same time, don't let him push you into something you don't feel ready for.

• Do not share everything with him without exception.

Sharing your own life with your partner and exchanging ideas regularly is a natural part of a happy relationship. However, you shouldn't overdo it, because if you tell each other everything without exception, you'll not only eventually run out of things to say, but you'll quickly become un-interesting. If you take it slower, you'll still have plenty of time to share details of your lives with each other.

• Don't be jealous of his ex-girlfriend.

The topic of ex-partners can be a sensitive one at the beginning, especially if the last relationship ended not so long ago. However, there is no point in being jealous of his ex-girlfriend, because what's over is over. Even if he is still in contact with her, it is not necessarily a bad sign for you. It is possible to have a friendship after a relationship has ended, especially if the breakup was further in the past. Excessive jealousy can massively jeopar-dize a relationship, so beware of making this mistake, and if necessary, talk to your (potential) partner about it if you are seriously worried.

• Don't pretend.

You sometimes do a lot to please another person, and this can even go as far as completely pretending to like something even though it is not true. It is good for a relationship if both partners each have their own interests that they can pursue separately. So be authentic and don't pretend to be different than you are, because sooner or later it will be exposed anyway. A woman who pursues and represents her own interests looks much more attractive than such a woman who is only looking for external recognition.

• Lack of respect is a relationship killer that you should avoid.

Lack of respect is a huge problem in a relationship and usually creeps in slowly after a long time. A big mistake you should not make is to show him too little respect before or at the beginning of a relationship. So you should accept his limits and not exceed them. A "no" means "no" and should be respected in all situations.

• Don't ask questions that are too intimate.

This mistake is mainly related to his ex-partners. There are nicer things for you to talk about than his ex-girlfriends. You should also avoid talking about ex-boyfriends all the time and focus on what lies ahead for the two of you with your potential new partner.

WHAT ELSE YOU SHOULD CONSIDER

It is much easier to do something instead of not doing something. That is, it is easier for us to adopt positive behaviors rather than frantically trying to prevent another behavior. While it's important to be aware of potential pitfalls and mistakes at the beginning of a relationship, you should focus primarily on the positives and consider what good things you can contribute to your relationship. In the chaos of emotions and probably floating on cloud nine, you can quickly forget the essentials and be blinded by your feelings. For this reason, this section contains a few more tips to give you a good example.

• Talk about commonalities and values you share.

Shared values are an important part of a basis for the relationship. Our values are closely related to the needs we have, and widely differing needs are known to be a frequent cause of separation. You can only counteract this if you first become aware of your own values. What plays a central role for you in a relationship? Is it freedom? Trust? Honesty? Caring? The list can go on endlessly. It is also advisable to actually make a list of your values and have your partner do the same. This way you can compare your values and start talking about them. However, you should be able to explain what each value means to you, as each term can be interpreted differently. Talk about your similarities and differences, and consider which values specifically play an important role in your relationship.

• Keep your spaces.

As you know, it is a fatal mistake to take your partner by surprise in a fresh relationship and not give him or her any more space. For this reason, it is helpful if you sit down together and talk about what space you want to give each other and keep. You should respect your partner's space and give yourself enough time to take care of your own business. If you keep this in mind from the beginning, you will avoid conflict arising later from feelings of lack of attention.

• Take plenty of time to get to know each other.
Or in other words, be aware that really getting to know each other can be a long process. You can learn something new about your partner even after months or even years and understand them better that way. That's why you don't have to stress at all in the beginning and try to understand each other as well and as quickly as you can. If it fits between you, you have enough time for this, which you should also take.

• Be honest with each other.
Of course, you want to show your best side, especially in the initial phase. Sometimes you may feel the need to hide certain facts about your past, for example, because you fear that this could have a negative impact on your partner's image of you. It also takes a lot of trust to tell each other certain things, but your partner will certainly listen to you carefully and not judge you. After all, your past

has made you the person he wants to be with to-day.

• Communicate openly with each other.
Communicating openly with each other is usually easier said than done, but if you consciously agree to speak openly when the other person is doing something that bothers you, you will get better at it and eventually do it automatically. In this way, you will prevent a negative emotional pile-up that could suddenly burst at some point with dire consequences, and instead work to find solutions to the minor or major difficulties. In addition, you should not only talk openly about the negative matters, but also about those that have triggered a good feeling in you. In this way, you can eliminate the bad step by step and strengthen the good, har-monious togetherness.

• Clarifies important questions.
There are things or experiences that you know you want to share with your partner sooner or la-ter. Even if you should not take him by surprise or even force him to do something, such topics should be addressed openly. Just because you're

already talking about meeting each other's parents today doesn't mean it has to happen tomorrow. Take your time, but always talk openly about your wishes and plans, as long as they directly affect your partner.

Making men happy in a relationship

A happy relationship is a high goal for most people. It means having a partner by your side that you can rely on, with whom you go through good times and bad, support each other and spend beautiful moments together. But a happy relationship doesn't just happen when two compatible people find each other and decide to enter into a partnership. The fact that you basically complement and understand each other is one thing, but the other is that a happy relationship also takes a lot of effort and work. However, once you've managed to establish healthy behaviors, you'll notice that all the work you've put in pays off.

A happy relationship requires happy partners, and what's the quickest and easiest way to make sure you're happy together? You can do that by trying to make your partner happy. So how you can make sure that you have a happy man by your side, who in return wants to make you equally happy, you shall learn in detail in this chapter.

WHAT MATTERS IN A HAPPY RE-LATIONSHIP?

First of all, let's ask ourselves what constitutes a happy relationship in the first place. This phrase "happy relationship" is so easy to say that we think we know the true meaning behind it. Some may think that in a happy relationship there is never any arguing, but I say that is wrong. For others, the term may mean spending every free minute with your partner and sharing beautiful moments together. While this can also be part of happy partnerships, relationships are usually quite complex and they cannot be turned around from an unhappy to a happy relationship and vice versa by a single factor. The aspects that contribute to a good relationship are very diverse.

1. Balance

You surely know the Taijitu, a symbol from the philosophy of Yin and Yang, which stands for two opposites, which combined together result in a harmonious unity. It should be the same with a relationship, because here too, at least to some extent, two very different people can meet. The art of living together in harmony is to remain in balance and not to go to extremes that could strain the relationship. For a balanced relationship, a balanced mind is a real helper, because it allows the partners to argue on the one hand, but to reconcile again, to spend a lot of time together, but also to take it easy sometimes and enjoy the time alone.

Balance and harmony also mean that compromises must be made, because even if two people agree on many things, disagreements will arise from time to time. In these situations, one of the two should not try to impose his or her will, but instead negotiate with a lot of willingness to compromise.

2. Safety and reliability - being a safe haven for the partner

Giving your partner security in a relationship means sticking to your agreements and standing by when your partner is not doing well or needs support. This mutual support gives each other a feeling of security, as if the partner were a safe haven on which one can always rely. Acting in a way that gives your partner a sense of security not only fulfills an important human need for that same security, but also ensures that there is a basis for a long and happy partnership.

3. The right communication as a basic prerequisite

Couples who communicate openly and regularly with each other address problems in a timely manner, thus eliminating them and avoiding relationship crises in the future. If they don't, unexpressed feelings, thoughts and concerns are pent up and swept under the rug, which can have devastating consequences for the relationship. This can mean dissatisfaction and insecurities about the partnership, flings or a breakup. So taking the time to discuss even small things together can raise the relationship quality tremendously. The relatively open, inquisitive way of dealing with each other, especially when first getting to know each other, should be carried over into the partnership communication as far as possible.

But if this is missed, it is not the end of the world, because everything can be learned and worked out together. With a little practice with your partner, you will then also be able to address even difficult topics and talk about them calmly. This will prevent you from not being attentive to each other's feelings and losing the emotional bond, on the contrary - you will strengthen your cohesion and your ability to talk about anything in the future.

4. Honesty and trust

Values such as honesty and trust together form an unbeatable team, which paves the way for a happy relationship as an important relationship aspect. Lies have short legs. Those couples who focus on honest communication know this, because they know that it would harm themselves if they were dishonest with their partner. Honesty is a matter of respect, which is also essential in a good partnership. After all, with honesty there can be no distrust, nor jealousy, which can massively damage a relationship if it gets out of hand.

If you are honest with your partner, you automatically develop a strong trust in each other, which gives you the security and peace of mind to keep your cool even in difficult times. But be careful: A partner who has once been caught lying is not easily trusted again. Trust must be built up slowly but surely, but it can be lost quickly and must be regained just as slowly and laboriously.

5. Sex as an important aspect
Physical intimacy is also not to be neglected as a component of a good relationship. During sex, the body releases the bonding hormone oxytocin, which strengthens the feeling of connection and togetherness. The frequency plays less and less of a role in the course of a relationship, because the quality is the decisive factor. Sex not only makes people happy, it should also be fun and not just a boring routine. However, the topic also harbors risks of conflict, for example, if one partner feels the need for sex more often, is not satisfied, is even in pain, or simply finds it boring.

Communication about this can also help, because in fact it often fails due to a lack of exchange about one's own wishes and needs. However, there are times when physical closeness takes a back seat in favor of other things, and even then there is no reason to worry, because sex is an important aspect of relationships, but not the central one.

6. Free time spent together
Shared experiences bring you closer together, they create conversation and memories for the future. It's a great feeling to be able to share an interest with your partner or try completely new things that move two people forward as a couple. Time spent together in a meaningful way strengthens the quality of the relationship and ultimately with it the feeling of satisfaction.

7. Celebrate your love
A partnership, let alone a happy one, cannot be taken for granted. To appreciate and honor this, couples who want to continue to stay happy together should regularly take the time to celebrate their love. An anniversary is a great opportunity

for this, but you shouldn't limit the celebration to just one day a year. If it can be arranged, you can make it a weekly ritual where you consciously make time for each other. This can be a romantic date or a simple walk, the main thing is to show each other that your partner is valued.

8. The partner as best friend

What is better than having a loving partner? Even better is to have a loving partner who is also your best friend. Being a good team with your partner on a friendship level is also a huge benefit for a relationship, because it usually makes the people involved see their partner as their biggest confidant. Someone with whom you can talk about everyday things, but also sink into deep conversations for hours over a glass of wine, has the potential for a lasting happy relationship.

9. Opposites attract?

Opinions on whether it is better to have a partner who is as similar as possible in all respects or who should be completely different from you are quite divergent. The fact is that certain contrasts can definitely create tension, positive tension that can inspire each other to try new things and deal with new things. For some people, too much harmony in this respect would be boring, while for others it would be unbearable in the long run with a partner who shares completely different preferences. What is important in all of this, however, is that there is a certain basic consensus.

This consensus should primarily relate to questions such as "What are my values?", "How do I want to live?", "What are my goals?". For all the beautiful, inspiring tension that exists otherwise, fundamentally divergent needs and desires will only be able to lead to an unsatisfied relationship in the long run. After all, there's no real way to compromise on matters like family planning or marriage, which inevitably means that at least one of the two will be unhappy if their desires differ. So to ensure that this basis of certain fundamental beliefs is in place, the situation between you should be examined as early as possible.

10. Live and let live

A happy relationship and trying to change your partner simply don't go together. Instead, mutual acceptance and tolerance in all matters is part of it. Even in situations where a couple is of completely opposite opinion, they must be respectful of each other and should not be made to feel that their partner is not good enough or needs to be fundamentally changed. After all, both parties have voluntarily decided to enter into a relationship, so the partner should also be accepted as he is. Apart from that, it also feels much better for oneself not to constantly criticize the partner, but to face each other with a lot of love and acceptance.

11. A similar sense of humor

Laughter is healthy and makes you happy, and for a relationship this is even more true, because laughing together strengthens the bond. When laughing, the body releases happiness hormones that provide a sense of well-being, and this accordingly has a very positive effect on a partnership. The more similar the humor, the higher the probability of sharing these happy moments with each other to the fullest. For example, watching a funny movie together can be a way to laugh more together, but be careful if your partner has a different sense of humor than you do, this could lead to incomprehension.

12. Self-love as the basis for love for the partner
You will have heard that you have to love yourself before you can love another person. Self-love is a complex issue and, depending on your starting point, can be difficult to achieve, so this doesn't mean that you have to be one hundred percent satisfied with everything about yourself before you should enter into a relationship.

But basically it can be said that a negative self-image usually has just as negative an effect on relationships of all kinds, because the bad feelings are thereby transferred to other people. For example, extreme self-doubt can lead to someone transferring these doubts and dissatisfaction to their partner, which can result in jealousy that endangers the relationship. Especially after separations, but also again and again in between and in the middle of a relationship, it is therefore important to practice self-love, because yes, self-love is something you can build up step by step, but more about that later.

13. Taking and giving freedom

Free space for own hobbies and friends is incredibly important in a relationship, although it is also very nice to spend time together with your partner. But you have to remember that both people are still independent, should have their own lives and interests, hobbies and contacts. If you as a couple constantly just squat on each other, you don't even have the opportunity to miss the other person. By taking this space, however, you appreciate the relationship all the more and you have something exciting to talk about afterwards. So everyone should take this space and above all not let it be taken, that is, each partner must give the other the same space. Wanting to restrict the partner to this extent, for reasons of jealousy or the like, will sooner or later lead to a major crisis and probably also to a separation.

14. Willingness to compromise

The willingness to compromise is essential for a harmonious partnership. This involves putting one's own wishes and needs aside and negotiating them in a spirit of partnership. Pleasing the other person can be just as nice as fulfilling one's own wishes, but above all it creates balance among each other. It should be noted, however, that this never goes against one's own values or deepest desires, because this will also not work in the long run.

15. Surprises

Especially after years in a relationship, it is the small or bigger surprises that keep love fresh and exciting. These can be planned activities or outings, the main thing is to show your partner that you put effort and thought into it. In this way, boredom is kept away, while the love and connection between you is strengthened.

16. Be able to forgive

Arguing from time to time is just as much a part of a relationship as spending good times together. However, the decisive factor here is that you should be able to forgive your partner afterwards. This requires that both partners really want to maintain the relationship and are willing to work on themselves.

Certainly, there will be individually specific things that make a relationship a truly happy and fulfilling one in the first place. However, the points mentioned above form a basis that can be applied to virtually any partnership. If a couple knows their own values, they will also know what really matters to them in the relationship. It can also help to simply talk to your partner about what a perfect relationship should look like.

SO HE STAYS BY YOUR SIDE

There's no doubt that it's nice to have found a partner with whom everything feels right at first and with whom you can simply have a really fulfilling, happy relationship. Basically, then, there's no reason to worry that he might leave you overnight, unless perhaps he has very serious commitment issues or other problems. Nevertheless, you want your partner to stay by your side for a long time and, above all, be happy with you and the relationship. But how do you go about it?

Unless there is serious concern that your relationship may soon be over, reflect on the positive things that are already going very well between you. Reread the aspects of a happy relationship, asking yourself to what extent you are already fulfilling these points and what you could work on. Keep in mind that a happy relationship doesn't just come about and be kept alive completely effortlessly, but requires a lot of work, time and effort. This also means that you really want this relationship, because only then you are also willing to invest all this work.

For example, if you notice that you haven't done anything exciting to keep your partnership exciting and fresh for a very long time, but have just been sitting on the couch most evenings, it's time to have a talk with your partner and plan an outing. Also, clearly express that it is important to you to spend quality time together, as you care about your relationship and want both of you to be satisfied. Alternatively, you can plan small surprises or give him a small gift. It may be that the life of the relationship together gets a little out of sight at times and you need to focus on something else, but this is exactly the wrong time to blame your partner. So, by showing that you are making an effort, your partner will return the same attention to you, if he or she cares about your relationship as much as you do.

Sometimes, however, your partner may withdraw a bit and you fear that this will soon mean the end between you. As mentioned in the chapter on distancing, there is often no serious cause for concern when your partner seeks to withdraw. Listen to your gut feeling and if it tells you that something is wrong, stay calm at first and try to reach out to your partner and seek a conversation. Keep the conversation open and don't accuse your partner of not wanting the relationship or of not making an effort. There is really no place for such accusations in a relationship.

Instead, ask him what he might want, what his needs are right now, and then talk about how you can balance your respective needs. General doubts about a relationship are not uncommon and are not necessarily dangerous. What's important in all of this is that you don't close yourselves off to each other, question your own behavior, especially if it's already come to blows, and recognize warning signs. Your gut feeling is usually a good indicator of these warning signs, which indicate when something is not quite going right in your partnership at the moment. In these situations, you should try to look at the situation as objectively as possible and also try to talk to your partner.

COMMON HOBBIES

A person's hobbies are probably one of the first things you ask about when you first meet that person. Rightly so, because a hobby or a special interest says a lot about a person in the vast majority of cases. Maybe you even got to know each other through a common hobby, such as sports or a concert or other public event that represents a certain interest? In this case, in any case, you have already found a common ground to talk about and exchange, but it is not uncommon that the hobbies of a couple can differ greatly.

There can really be more important and decisive things than the same hobbies. It is much more important that you share the same values and have the same plans and goals for the future. For example, what good would it do if you both like to watch movies or play sports, but one wants to start a family and the other doesn't? It's hard to compromise on important issues that affect your life, but you can live very well with different interests.

On the other hand, sharing a hobby can be a wonderful way to continue strengthening your bond. Especially if you're not planning a family together, it's important to still take care of projects that keep you busy. You have the option of either sharing one of his hobbies or one of yours, or you can find an entirely new hobby to explore together. Both have their advantages. Taking on a hobby that your partner is already invested in gives you an easier way to get started right away. Plus, you're getting into something that might never have been interesting to him or you originally, but for your partner, you're known to be willing to do quite a bit.

Alternatively, you can find a hobby that you both haven't had anything to do with yet. In this way, both of you will get to know something new and work on it together, which will bring you closer together and certainly give you a lot of pleasure. The new hobby will give you a good reason to spend more valuable time together and not just waste it senselessly.

Hobbies for couples

Just finding a new hobby that your partner also wants to share with you sounds easier said than done. It doesn't have to be something incredibly big, spectacular or special, because the main thing is that you both enjoy it. However, finding ideas can be a little tricky, so below you'll find a list of hobbies that work well for couples.

Hobbies for home

Especially in bad weather or when it gets colder outside, home hobbies are wonderful for doing something against boredom. The possibilities are almost endless.

• Save money

Admittedly, this sounds like an incredibly stuffy and boring hobby at first. But saving together can be a lot of fun and is especially useful if you already share a household. The two of you can think about how you want to save money and find out what you really need to live. Maybe you'll notice how much money you regularly spend on things that aren't really necessary? In this way, you can save a considerable amount of money each month and spend it on more enjoyable things, such as a vacation together.

• Prepare cocktails
Delicious cocktails can be not only in the bar, but also at your home. It can be a lot of fun to try new recipes together and enjoy unusual creations. Even for those who do not drink alcohol, there are alternatives. Let yourself be inspired and have a great time.

• Fathom your childhoods
When showing children's photos or old video footage, one or the other laugh is guaranteed. You're sure to have forgotten a lot about your own past and can reminisce in these moments and, above all, get to know each other better. You may be surprised what new things you will learn about your partner.

• Play board games
Many people still know board games from their childhood and have long forgotten them after all these years. It can be so good to just play with

someone again and forget everything else, but also to challenge each other and laugh a lot. There is a wide range of board games for two, so the possibilities are almost limitless and there is guaranteed to be something for everyone.

• Baking and cooking together
Preparing delicious food together kills two birds with one stone: on the one hand, this hobby brings you closer together and you spend more valuable time together, and on the other hand, the previously cooked or baked can be eaten together with pleasure. You should take the time to try out some unusual dishes that you might not otherwise dare to try.

• Remodel the apartment
If you share a household, a joint home makeover can be a great project. Get rid of the items you've grown tired of, or give them a new coat of paint, or otherwise change them. This way, you can create a living space that you both feel comfortable in and enjoy living in.

• Clean out and sell old

In the course of remodeling your apartment, it is also a good idea to clean it out. After all this time, you can accumulate unused items that only take up space. If you can't use them anymore, you should sell them or give them away. Having fewer unnecessary items lying around is definitely a liberating feeling. With the money you make, you can afford to go on a nicc trip.

• Discover new music

The musical offerings out there are immense and varied. If the two of you are at least a little interested in music, it can be fun to search for new artists or genres together. There are plenty of radio programs or playlists to listen to on the Internet, but digging out old music cassettes or CDs can also bring you great joy.

• Create a common blog

Creating a blog on the Internet about a special interest will definitely bring you closer together. It's nice to slowly watch the project grow and learn new things along the way.

Sports hobbies

Sport is a popular hobby among couples. Many of them set their sights on getting fitter, losing weight or simply doing something for their health. Whatever you choose, you can't go wrong with joint exercise, because it's good for you and your relationship.

• Dance

Even for the sporty or those who think they can't dance, this can still be a great new hobby to get to know your partner. Dancing invigorates your relationship immensely and improves your body image. You can go to a dance school or take a class, or simply try to teach yourself.

• Fitness training

This type of workout can be completely customized. Whether you decide to go to the gym or prefer to work out at home or outdoors with your own body weight is up to you. The important thing is that you motivate and push each other. This way, you not only have a lot of fun together, but you also do something for your health at the same time.

- Acro Yoga

This form of yoga is a workout specifically desig-
ned for two people. Be inspired to try this couple
yoga and try something new, even if you should
approach slowly. This way you can train body and
mind together.

- Crossminton

Also known as speed badminton, this sport com-
bines elements of badminton, squash and tennis to
create a completely new game. The playing field
can be almost anywhere outdoors or in a hall. All
you need then is the appropriate equipment and
off you go!

Relaxing together

Relaxation can't be a hobby? But of course it can. Relaxing together with your partner and getting away from the stress of everyday life is even better than relaxing alone.

• Hiking

A hiking tour through nature is balm for the soul and good for the body. Find a nice destination and hike there together. Such a tour offers the opportunity to have deep conversations or just listen to the sounds of nature and really relax.

• Canoeing

Such a canoe ride in the water can also be very relaxing in nice weather for two. You can either rent a canoe or buy a cheap inflatable canoe.

• Watch series

Enjoying a series together can be a great alternative to the usual television program. Grab some snacks and get cozy. Even though this is a passive hobby, it can give you additional conversation material.

• Wellness

Treat yourself to a visit to the sauna or go for a relaxing swim in the spa. You can also plan a wellness day at home and really enjoy yourself.

• Discover museums

There are museums for all kinds of focuses and interests. You will certainly find something that suits both of you. So you can learn new things and see exciting things in a mostly quiet, pleasant atmosphere.

• Meditate

Meditation has been proven to have many positive effects on our body and mind. It's not about thinking about nothing, but consciously not evaluating your thoughts, but noticing them. If you meditate together with your partner, you spend this time in a very special way. You can either meditate freely or start a guided meditation.

Joint projects

Joint projects give you a chance to be creative and strengthen your cohesion. A long-term project gives you something to watch grow. It gives you a lot to talk about and good reasons to spend more time together.

• A joint photo project

No matter what your goal, whether it's a special photo series or a calendar, getting creative together is twice as much fun as going it alone. The possibilities of motifs and techniques are many. You can start with what you have and then invest in better equipment.

• Implement DIY ideas

With your own craft projects, you can spend time together in a meaningful and productive way. Maybe you want a small new piece of furniture, but haven't gotten around to buying it yet? Try building it yourself instead. But smaller projects can be fun, too.

• Give a seminar

Maybe not the #1 hobby you think of as a couple, but if you happen to be very knowledgeable in a certain area, taking a class at the community college can be a nice project to do together.

• Plan vacations and trips

Planning trips together may sound almost too obvious, but it's the special trips that you should dedicate yourselves to. How about a short day trip or short vacation to a place you wouldn't otherwise choose? Broaden your horizons and learn something new.

• Support charitable projects

If you both want to do something good for the world together, you can join a charity project or start something yourself.

• A common pet

Getting a pet wants to be well thought out, as this requires a lot of responsibility, time and possibly money, but a pet can bring you a lot of joy beyond that and be something that really bonds you together.

• Learn something new

Have you always wanted to learn a certain language or skill, but you could never find the time? As a couple, you can motivate and support each other.

• Expand your comfort zone

Expanding your comfort zone can take a lot of effort and be a real challenge. On the other hand, expanding this zone helps you to grow beyond yourselves. You become stronger individually, but also as a couple, because you learn to trust yourselves more. The ways to expand your comfort zone are very individual, as everyone has their own comfort zone, but working together you can give each other support and encouragement.

The list of common hobbies could be continued endlessly. In the end, it's up to you to decide what you'll enjoy. It's worth trying something completely new, even if you think it's not for you. Maybe you'll discover a new passion, or maybe you'll be smarter and know what you definitely don't like. In any case, it is important to get involved with new things and especially with your partner. Two of you have more ideas than one person alone, so inspire each other and do not be afraid to make suggestions to the other. You have nothing to lose, only a lot to gain.

CONSISTENCY AND FREEDOM

The elements of consistency and space are important for everyone in a relationship, not just for men. Consistency means the feeling of security and a constant intensity on an emotional, but also sexual level. So someone who wants a lasting partnership doesn't want to have to experience constant ups and downs or be confronted with constant doubts on the part of their partner, even though it is in a way normal to go through ups and downs together in a long-lasting relationship. The freedom you should nevertheless take for yourself and give to the other person may seem to contrast with closeness and consistency, but they are at least as important if a relationship is to last. You should definitely strive for these values if you want a harmonious and fulfilling relationship.

What leads to lasting relationships
Psychologist John Gottmann used experiments he conducted and evaluated over a period of 40 years to explore how to quickly and fairly accurately predict whether a couple has the potential to have a lasting relationship. To do this, Gottmann set up

a love lab in a one-bedroom apartment in Seattle, equipped with everything needed to live. Over the course of 40 years, the psychologist observed more than 3,000 couples in this apartment who volunteered to be watched as they talked, argued and lived together. With the help of cameras, the couples' facial expressions, gestures and reactions were recorded in detail. In addition, individual people were wired up to record reactions such as their pulse or sweating on the palms of their hands. From these parameters, Gottmann not only developed groundbreaking insights, but also his relationship formula, which he believed would lead to a lasting partnership.

Using a 15-minute video in which a couple talked about their relationship and addressed points of contention, Gottmann was then able to predict with a hit probability of 94% whether the relationship of the couple in question had the potential to be a long and happy one. The psychologist developed the so-called Dow Jones Index, for which a total of 20 different parameters are offset against each other. For example, a positive effect on this index would be if a couple actively sought closeness to each other. Whether two people in a relationship would be positive towards each other can be well proven by how they deal with each other non-verbally, i.e. happy couples automatically send each other more positive signals.

Couples therapist and psychologist Dr. Ilka Vasterling talks about another formula that is crucial for maintaining a harmonious relationship: love and conflict should be in a ratio of five to one. So if a nasty comment slips out in an argument, it should be balanced out with five loving gestures. The same can also be applied to the joint conversation, i.e. after a negative signal, five additional positive signals should always be sent. Certainly, one does not always have the head to recount such things in the middle of a conversation or argument. It is rather a matter of always remembering to remain kind to your partner even in times of conflict and to give kind words or gestures.

In addition to too many negative signals, Gottmann also sees disloyalty as a major danger for relationships. Infidelity doesn't always have to mean cheating; it can also occur when a partner puts something such as his or her own career above the relationship. Selfish behavior and injustice have just as much to do with infidelity, says

Gottmann. So what is the solution to this? Only trust can lead to a lasting relationship and even restore a broken relationship. Trust may be an elusive, abstract concept for most, but Gottmann claims it can even be calculated and targeted and studied.

For this, he says, it is especially important to see trust and loyalty as **the** basic pillars of a relationship, contrary to many other opinions that claim that trust is just one of many aspects. Couples with a good basis of trust cooperate with each other and respond to the other person instead of wanting to win in a conflict themselves. They know that there are certain conflicts that they can only solve and eliminate together. If there is genuine trust and love between the couple, they want the best for their partner and therefore do not wait for him to give in to a dispute. Finally, you can have the greatest success as a couple only if you take into account each other's wishes and empathize with them. By being considerate of each other, you will get the best possible outcome for the individual.

Giving each other space has just as much to do with consideration and a healthy relationship, because space is also related to trust and the desire for consistency. A harmonious partnership requires not only a strong "we" feeling, but also a good "I" feeling. Often, different needs come into conflict: one person would prefer to spend all their time with their partner, while the other would like to have more space for themselves or other areas of their life. The following tips will show you how to create space between you.

1. First take a look at yourself

Many problems in relationships start with the individual, because unresolved inner emotional conflicts are then transferred to the partnership. Ask yourself honestly if you are insecure or jealous. There is no shame in admitting that we have insecurities, because pretty much everyone does. The trick is to admit them to yourself and work on not letting those insecurities put you down. Often insecurity arises from past hurts that we have unconsciously remembered. It then serves as a kind of protective reaction, but usually hinders us in everyday life more than it actually helps us. In relationships, it also often leads to one person starting to cling and driving the partner into distance with this behavior. A vicious circle that you can break if you are affected by it.

The best remedy is to talk openly with your partner about such insecurities and fears. If he is the one who is plagued by great insecurity, you should try to understand his fears and respond accordingly by lovingly explaining to him that your need for space has nothing to do with a lack of love for him.

2. Give the term a positive meaning

The word free space should not evoke negative associations from the beginning of your relationship, if possible. Unfortunately, this often happens after arguments, when your partner's need for space is seen as a punishment. However, it should not be a break in the relationship, but something that is an essential part of the relationship and belongs to it as well as the time spent together.

You should see space in a relationship as something positive, because it gives you plenty of time for yourself, your hobbies and interests. In order not to lose yourselves in the "we" feeling and still be able to spend a happy future together, it is important that you see freedom as a great opportunity.

3. Find your own hobby each

You have received enough examples of common hobbies. The point here is that you should have hobbies that you do not pursue together, but separately. You should find time for them at least once a week, because it is important that you keep your independence and expect the same from your partner. Partners who have interests outside of their relationship are also much more attractive to each other.

4. Stay true to yourself

Staying true to yourself despite everything in a relationship is not to be underestimated for maintaining healthy space. You should also not expect your partner to give up certain behavior and thinking just because you are now a couple. In what is important for you personally and what makes you as a person, you should not bend under any circumstances. In this way, you will prevent yourself from constricting each other or yourselves, because after all, the goal should not be to change, but to enrich.

5. Value your friendships

Maintaining friendships alongside a relationship is incredibly important. After all, if you don't take care of your friends, they will gradually turn away from you and you will lose contact with them. So the fewer friends you have, the more you tend to cling to your partner even more, which is not good for the relationship at all in the long run. Avoid this together with your partner by consciously taking time for your friendships. This automatically creates free spaces that can have an insanely harmonious effect on your relationship.

The requirements for a balanced partnership can actually be broken down to a few things. Trust and respect play a very important role if you want to have a happy and stable relationship in which you have enough space to develop yourself as an individual. Problem solving or building mutual trust and respect usually always starts with the individual, with yourself and with your partner. With enough self-reflection and good communication with your partner, together you will definitely be able to build a stable foundation for a long-lasting, happy relationship.

DESIRE AND SEXUAL ATTRACTION

Sexuality remains without question a central topic even in long-term relationships. In order for you and your partner to remain happy together in the long run, it is therefore important not to disregard this point. Many people think that it is inevitable that sexual attraction and passion will flatten out over time and that you have to put up with it. However, constantly living with a sense of suffering when you are unbalanced with your partner in terms of sexuality cannot contribute to a good relationship in the long run.

There is no need to panic immediately during phases of sexual unwillingness. For reasons such as illness or stress at work, it is legitimate to initially put the physical desire for the partner in a relationship on the back burner. It becomes problematic, however, when the lack of interest lasts and results in great dissatisfaction on both sides. The difficulty here is that it is usually a gradual process and therefore difficult to see through when the different needs for physical intimacy become a serious problem. It is usually the case that a person suffers from his or her lack of desire, or else feels sexually undesirable. Both situations are hardly bearable over a longer period of time and therefore not infrequently lead to separation.

In our society, the idea that this process will inevitably run its course at some point seems to be very common. In any case, the fact is that almost half of all Germans are dissatisfied with their sex lives. Is the flattening of desire perhaps not so inevitable after all? What can be done about it?

A creeping process
At the beginning of a relationship, the topic of sex is rarely a major point of contention. In the infatuation phase, when everything is still new and exciting, three hormones in particular contribute to the fact that we can't keep our hands off each other. On the one hand, dopamine plays a role, because the happiness hormone ensures strong feelings of happiness. Secondly, oxytocin comes into play, which creates the feeling of bonding. Last

but not least, the effect of testosterone also comes into play, which makes us feel self-confident and confident. This mixture of hormones is abundant in the early stages of a relationship, which is why sex life is usually perceived as very satisfying at that time.

What then happens is that the daily grind gradually creeps into relationship life and mutual attraction may still be present, but sex life is no longer perceived as particularly exciting. However, the oxytocin continues to have its effect and has created the feeling of bonding, but it also gives the couple a kind of false sense of security, as they then often think they no longer have to make an effort for their partner. Even if the sexual desire for each other does not completely subside, it can still lead to routines that are just as unfulfilling in the long run as if there were no intimacy at all between the couple anymore.

Sex as a mirror of a relationship
Whether things are going well in a relationship in general can be seen in a couple's sex life. That is, the more partners turn to each other, pay

attention to each other, send positive signals and touch each other, the greater the likelihood that this will have a positive effect on their sex life. However, if partners hardly notice each other, no longer listen to each other and hardly seek physical contact, this will logically have negative consequences for sexual desire. This is to say that sexual desire and desire and the loss of it should not be considered alone, but should always be seen in a larger context. By both of you striving for a fulfilling sex life, you cannot sweep aside all the other building blocks of your relationship, but sex is fundamentally an important building block that in itself can say a lot about the whole.

At this point, I would like to talk about trust again, because a lack of trust in the partner is a common reason for sexual disinterest. This mistrust does not necessarily have to be rooted in the current relationship, but can also have to do with previous painful experiences. The feeling of having been cheated on or otherwise having experienced infidelity is not pretty. It can leave such a lasting mark on a person that healthy trust with the current partner can only be built with difficulty. But even in current relationships, mistrust can be caused by disappointments or simply by breaches of trust of all kinds. Here it is important to re-establish this trust in each other, and to do this a couple must learn to forgive and talk about the negative experiences and feelings. Only when you are at peace with yourselves and as a couple can you let go and enjoy carefree intimacy.

Stimulate sexual attraction

The good news is that yes, you can do something to maintain sexual desire and restore it if it has been lost. The following tips will show you how you can do this with your partner.

• Eliminate conflicts and take care of your relationship

Unresolved conflicts and relationship problems interfere with the desire for each other, so you should start here first. Even small disputes accumulate over time if they are not talked about, and thus gradually affect the general mood between you. Show each other that you value each other and that you really care about each other. If you have major relationship problems that are difficult to deal with on your own, couples therapy may be worthwhile.

• Remember your first phase of infatuation
Pretty sure lack of sexual attraction was not an issue between you at the beginning of your relationship. After all, everything was still new and exciting, and you enjoyed spending time together and showing affection. Now it's time to think back to that phase. Ideally, make a list that you fill with behaviors that distinguished your infatuation phase. What did you do together and how hard did you care for your partner? These reflections should help you reintegrate these behaviors into your relationship to give it a breath of fresh air.

• Avoids too much proximity
Avoiding too much closeness is not counterproductive, but enormously important to maintain a certain balance in the relationship. You should be recognizable as individuals and clearly differentiate yourselves from each other. A person who leads his own life despite a fixed relationship immediately looks much more attractive.

• Work on your body image and feel attractive

Sexual attraction has a lot to do with charisma. Someone who is confident and simply feels beautiful and comfortable in their own skin can almost magically attract other people. However, feeling more attractive yourself is usually easier said than done, because it is a process that will probably take a little more time.

To feel more comfortable in your body, you should first consider what you may be unhappy with and what you can do to change that. Women are usually far too harsh on themselves when it comes to their external appearance, which depends on many factors. However, there is nothing wrong with wanting to optimize yourself a bit, as long as it is possible. A healthy body is usually the most attractive, but you should also pay attention to a healthy mind and self-image. Sometimes just dressing nicely is enough to make you feel more attractive, it is even said that wearing sexy underwear, even if it is not visible, acts like a real boost to your self-confidence.

• How strong are your needs actually?

Both partners should honestly ask themselves if sex is a priority for them in a relationship. If one of the two only gets involved in it in order not to jeopardize the relationship, it can't work in the long run. How big is your respective self-interest?

• What is your own sexual profile?

The sex researcher Ulrich Clement coined the term sexual profile. It is like an individual fingerprint, which is characterized by personal desires, needs and the general attitude towards sexuality. It is even advisable to become aware of the differences with your partner and to talk openly about unexpressed desires. From this new things can arise, which in turn can enormously increase the sexual attraction between you.

LOYALTY - AN ESSENTIAL VALUE

If people had to describe their ideal partner, the word "faithful" comes up in most cases. That a partner should be faithful is recognized by the general public as absolutely obvious, but rarely is the value of faithfulness given much thought. Having a faithful partner protects ourselves from disappointment, betrayal, and hurt, and by being faithful and loyal ourselves, we want to return the same sense of security to our partner. And yet, in relationships there are always cases of infidelity of various kinds. So, in order to have your partner happily by your side for as long as possible, it is not only important to be faithful yourself, but you should be able to expect the same from your partner. Let's take a closer look at this exciting topic.

Not cheating = fidelity?
If a partner cheats, we automatically see him or her as the exact opposite of a faithful person. But it's not only infidelity on a sexual level that poses a threat to relationships; emotional infidelity in particular is on the rise in relationships and leads to problems. Nevertheless, let's stay on the subject of cheating, because not cheating is not automatically faithfulness. Sounds paradoxical at first, but it's not.

Someone doesn't cheat, but thinks about it every day without putting the thoughts into action. Or one feels trapped in the social constraints and wants to live up to the expectations. But one can also have no sexual desire at all, no need for closeness. Is this faithful behavior towards the partner? Outwardly it is, but it is not active fidelity, but rather something that happens "by accident". Active fidelity, on the other hand, means making a conscious decision to work on oneself and the relationship, even though one might have plenty of opportunities to be unfaithful to one's partner.

The levels of fidelity
Fidelity is not a one-dimensional value that is characterized only by not getting into bed with another person. Instead, fidelity is a multi-faceted matter, which equally means that one can be unfaithful in multi-faceted ways. Women are generally more hurt by seeing their partner have a strong emotional connection with another woman, while men are more put off by the thought that their girlfriend might become sexually intimate with another man. Although it cannot be generalized, these are observations that can be made about the majority. However, the fact is that any

form of infidelity is unfair to the partner. The boundaries to infidelity are fluid here and certainly each person has his personal views that say when a partner would exceed its limits. Let's first take a look at the different levels of fidelity.

Emotional fidelity
One of the most important pillars of a relationship is emotional fidelity. It means that any emotional and non-sexual intimacy is treated exclusively and shared only with the partner. Certain things are shared only between partners and the affection given to each other includes only the partner. Those who are emotionally unfaithful have emotional affairs with others and thereby build closeness. Even if no physical cheating results, romantic feelings arise between the parties involved.

Typical signs of emotional infidelity:
• Someone shares emotional intimacy with another person. There is a lot of talk about experiences, adventures and feelings. Intimate secrets can also be shared.

• Contact with the third person is downplayed and how much time is actually shared with the person is downplayed.
• Talking about the partner with the other person, in the worst case talking badly about him.
• While there is no exchange of physical intimacy, the meetings proceed much like dates.
• The person concerned has too high expectations of the partner. If the partner does not meet this ideal, the search continues.

Social fidelity

Social fidelity in this case means not shifting the responsibility away from oneself if a relationship has gone to ruin. Blaming the ex-partner is generally not well received by a new partner, as this also has a similar effect to emotional infidelity.

Sexual fidelity

This form of fidelity means sharing certain physical intimacies only with one's partner. Depending on the definition, cuddling, kissing or having sex with another person is considered unfaithful. Even in polyamorous or open relationships, there may be boundaries that should definitely be discussed together.

Fidelity as an active decision

Being actively faithful to your partner means showing inner strength. To be faithful, one must be capable of commitment and have a certain emotional intelligence. Perseverance is also associated with fidelity, because in order to remain faithful in the long term and to go through difficult times together, you need the prerequisite that you do not lose sight of your long-term goals of the partnership. Infidelity, on the other hand, occurs when a situation in the relationship is seen as hopeless and one person has already distanced themselves emotionally from their partner. Sometimes people also cheat out of fear of getting too close. In this case, cheating is intended to reinforce the feeling of autonomy.

When you actively choose to be faithful to your partner, you are also actively doing something good for your relationship. It means staying true to your values and being aware of them. Faithfulness cannot be demanded, but it must arise from an inner need. In the end, you are not only being faithful to your partner, but also to yourself.

It can be easy to cross the boundaries in a partnership unnoticed when an initially platonic friendship gradually turns into an emotional affair. Accordingly, it is important to analyze the situation before it even comes to crossing the line. Even in difficult times, brief pleasure cannot be a solution. If you are unsure about where your respective boundaries lie, you should definitely talk about it openly so that you can have a healthy and happy relationship in good conscience.

A PARTNER WHO KNOWS WHAT SHE WANTS

One thing that every man wants in a committed relationship is a partner who knows what she wants. A relationship with a woman who knows what her goals are and what she wants out of a partnership is less complicated and more secure, because she is much less likely to change her mind from one moment to the next. You need to know that men who want a relationship that will last crave security. This is not exclusive to men, because after all, everyone wants a safe haven that he or she can always rely on. As a woman, if you can convey at the beginning of a relationship that you know where your expectations lie, you automatically give the impression of security that so many men desire.

But what does it even mean to know what you want? Especially when you're young, it's perfectly normal not to always be sure. How do I want to shape my life? Do I really want a long-term relationship now? Do I want to start a family later on? What are my values? All of these and many more are questions that can remain unanswered at first. It is also important to take the time to answer these questions for yourself before jumping into a relationship without having made prior arrangements. But regardless of whether you can already answer the important questions for yourself or not: certain qualities make a woman in the eyes of a man only real relationship potential. For example, this includes being able to have your own opinion and not just looking for confirmation from outside. You should know what is important to you in life and also stand up for it, be it a hobby, your friends or something that is especially close to your heart. In this way, you show your partner that you are authentic and won't let yourself be bent, because that's what a relationship is all about: consistency.

Wanting a woman who knows herself what she wants, in a way, also has something to do with consistency. A partner who is insecure about many things and prefers to be led by the opinions of others gives an equally insecure and volatile impression, because there is a possibility that she will eventually realize that what you have in common is not what she wants after all. It's difficult for a man to get involved in a long-term committed relationship with a woman if she fundamentally can't say what she wants her life to be like. Even if openness to new things is good, it is not conducive to a relationship to have no demands of your own.

It certainly helps if you have already gained some experience in relationship or dating other men, because this will sharpen your idea of what you really want in a partnership. You can see every experience as an enrichment, because they all help you to find your true desires and needs. Your ideas are also shaped by all possible areas of life and make you the unique person you are. Learning to become aware of these ideas, desires and needs will give you an equally clear advantage in your relationship life.

FAMILY

Whether you are single, in a relationship with or without children - you surely know that it is not easy to reconcile partnership and parenthood. The fact is, however, that many people still wish to start a family of their own. If you are single or have a partner but no children, it is not unlikely that the topic of starting a family will become a topic of conversation sooner or later. And it's enormously important to talk about it; after all, starting a family is not a decision you make over-night. Some people are already firmly convinced at an early age that they definitely want to have children at some point. If these people then also have a partner who feels the same way, there's basically not much to talk about at the beginning - you only have to think about the "when?" and "how?".

Other people, on the other hand, are not sure whether they want to have children. "Maybe later" is often the answer. It is perfectly legitimate to keep this question open as long as you are not one hundred percent sure. But when two people who are still uncertain about this enter into a relationship and want to maintain it in the long term, the topic of starting a family can also become a contentious issue. After all, indecision harbors the risk that both people will ultimately want something else and will not be able to reach a common denominator. Relationships largely consist of compromises, but when it comes to children, compromises cannot be agreed upon: Either you want to start a family or you don't. If either person becomes involved in something he or she never originally wanted, it can lead to major relationship problems and dissatisfaction.

How can you get around this dilemma? There is no guarantee, but it helps immensely to clarify such things early on or even before a relationship. After all, if you then realize that your wishes are simply too different, it's not too late to think things over in peace. Even though you may think that it is way too early to even talk about such things, it is better to at least ask. Having an open, noncommittal conversation about issues that could potentially concern you in the future can save you trouble later. It can also help you learn more about each other's life aspirations and ideas in general.

The topics of family, starting a family and couple relationships in families are very comprehensive and would - if discussed in detail - go beyond the scope of this book. One piece of advice that I would like to give you in any case, if you are still single, in a fresh relationship or one that has lasted a little longer, is that you or both of you should first make sure that you are on the same wavelength as far as these things are concerned. Only talking can help you get a feel for each other's desires and ideas. Even if you don't share one hundred percent of the same wishes, that doesn't have to mean the end for you, because through sensitive conversations and self-discovery, a solution can be found for many things that suits both of you.

Integrate the respective own family into the relationship life

Apart from starting a new family, each partner has their own family, namely parents, possibly siblings and still grandparents, nephews and nieces and many more. To some, family life is enormously important, while other people have gradually distanced themselves from their own family. Depending on how important being together and meeting family is to both of you, it may make sense to integrate each other into your own family life.

If your partner attaches great importance to family cohesion, he will certainly make an effort to introduce you to her or invite you to festivities. It is possible that the relationship between all parties involved will develop by itself, if you attach importance to it. But it still can't hurt to talk about it and ask if your partner even wishes to combine partnership and family life in such a way. A wonderful network of mutual help and support can come out of it, if both partners and families want it.

COMBAT EVERYDAY LIFE AND ROUTINES

There is hardly anything that makes a relationship more boring than the usual daily grind and routines. Although everyday life is also part of a partnership, it is an art not to let it get out of hand. After all, rigid routines can make a relationship not only boring and tiring, but even very unhappy. If you care about your partner and want to make them happy, you should take an active role in combating these routines and everyday life and create compensation for them. Below you will find tips on how to approach this.

1. Dates together

A good way to get away from the daily grind is to start dating regularly again. Set aside a day every week or at least every month to do something special again, whether it's a visit to a restaurant, the cinema, a concert, a club or an exhibition. Don't just leave everything to chance, but plan such meetings carefully in your calendar.

2. Talk to each other again

Of course, you communicate regularly on a day-to-day level and know roughly what's going on in each other's lives at the moment. But conversations that take place only in passing often remain superficial. So take the time again to just talk, about your feelings, fears, worries, thoughts. Without background noise and disturbances. This will not only bring you closer together, but also remind you regularly that you are not only spending your everyday life together, but that you are in a relationship together.

3. Agree on a cell phone ban

On the one hand, bans have no place in a happy relationship, but on the other hand, when a couple lives together, it happens far too often that both spend their evening together on the couch, but on the cell phone. Smartphones can be a real enrichment to life, but they can put a strain on relationship life if you are constantly distracted by them. So if you're spending the evening together, agree to respond only to urgent calls or messages after a certain time. This way you can focus your attention on each other and fill the time with more meaningful things.

4. Revel in beautiful memories together
The daily grind and routines usually mean that you take your partner for granted. By reminiscing and talking about beautiful memories together, you will also remember what you love about each other. Remember your infatuation phase and why you fell in love with each other. Beautiful photos or other mementos, such as from trips you took together, can help you do this.

5. Experience some action
The familiarity that grows between two people in a relationship after a while is a wonderful thing, however, it can also lead to a feeling of habit. You think you know practically everything about your partner and there's nothing exciting between you anymore. This is where the adrenaline comes in: When the two of you experience some action, it brings a breath of fresh air into your relationship. This can be a visit to the amusement park or escape room, or a new exciting sport. For those who

prefer a more leisurely pace, a trip to an unfamiliar area can be enough.

6. Say compliments and use small gestures
Saying a few kind words or showing nice gestures to your partner signals to them that you appreciate them. You can introduce as a ritual that you tell each other regularly, for example once a week, what you especially liked about your partner this week. What did he do that showed you he was the right partner for you? Sometimes it's just little everyday things that we appreciate, and other times it turns into a real confession of love.

7. Also focus on your own interests
Always doing everything together gets boring after a while. For more fresh air between you, you should also pursue your own hobbies, meet friends and simply spend time without your partner. This will make you much more happy to see each other again the next time.

8. Do not neglect the physical closeness
We're not just talking about sex, but also about physical contact, which you can incorporate into

your everyday life. It doesn't have to be just a hug or a kiss to greet and say goodbye, just take the time to hug, touch and exchange small caresses.

Let's talk about sex

Sex is an essential part of the relationship for most couples. How well it goes between you two in bed even generally reflects the current state between you. If the feeling of emotional closeness is lost and there is only arguing, this has a very negative effect on the desire for your partner. If, on the other hand, you lead a very harmonious partnership and also share physical tenderness in everyday life apart from sex, the probability of dissatisfaction in bed is lower. But what are men into and what can you do to have better experiences? We would like to approach these questions in this chapter.

WHAT MEN REALLY WANT IN BED

Men always want and can, besides they think of nothing else but sex. This is one of many clichés that exist on the subject of men and sex. In fact, men and women are not so different when it comes to desires and needs, but many false assumptions and prejudices still prevail.

A first interesting finding is that men care more about the woman's pleasure and satisfaction than you might think. In reality, men are into knowing that the woman is having fun and is totally blown away. In that sense, it also helps to tell him clearly what you're into, because men not only like women who know what they want in a relationship, but also those who know what they want during sex. Also, as I'm sure you know, men are into reassurance. It gives them a boost to the ego and spurs them on to new heights - even in bed. So let him know verbally if you like what he does. But stay authentic, because that comes across better than a posed, monotonous moan.

What men want

• Oral sex more often

Many women think that oral sex on a man is seen as a means to exercise power, but it is usually the other way around. Men like to surrender to a woman, to give her the position of power. After all, it also involves great trust, so watch what you do with your teeth.

• More Quickies

A spontaneous quickie is the perfect way to counteract the boring everyday life. Gladly even in more unusual places, men like it when women take the initiative and really take them by surprise. If you show him in this way how much you desire him, he will certainly weaken.

• Make out more often

You might think that men only want to kiss in order to secretly get what they actually want: Sex. But this is not necessarily true. Men also just like to kiss their partner. It's even better when the hands come into play and a lot of body contact is created.

• Let the woman take the lead

Many men wish to have sex in the riding position more often. Why? Compared to many other positions, this is one where they can relax for once and let the woman take the lead. You can choose the rhythm and intensity as you like, as long as you take care of your partner's best part to avoid nasty accidents.

• An extensive foreplay

Not only women want a good foreplay, because men it is just as important. Take your time to explore, caress and kiss. After all, it does not always have to go straight to the point.

• A threesome

That some men like to have a threesome with two women should be obvious. If a man finds a woman beautiful, two of them are an even better sight. But such games are certainly more suitable for singles, because as soon as at least one person is emotionally invested, it can lead to problems among themselves.

WHAT MEN DO NOT LIKE IN BED

• Women who do not drop during sex

If the partner is thinking about any problems or worries during sex, we notice that. Conversely, it's also very disturbing for men when they notice that their partner just can't let go. Therefore, try to turn off your thoughts for this time and focus your attention only on the two of you.

• Bitchiness

Bitchy behavior can be annoying, especially in bed. If you don't like something or don't feel like doing something in particular, you should express this in a normal tone.

• Uncertainty

Being insecure about one's own body is widespread among women and thus practically normal, but it is rather a hindrance during sex. Men do not notice small beauty flaws as we might think. If y-our partner wants to have sex with you, you can be sure that he wants you the way you are and not otherwise. Also, big insecurities only prevent you from being able to really enjoy and let yourself go.

If you are too worried about showing yourself in front of your partner, discuss your insecurities with him. He will almost certainly take away your insecurities and help you to accept yourself better.

MASTURBATION: HOW TO DIS- COVER YOUR FEMALE SEXUALITY

Masturbation is a topic that people rarely like to talk about openly. Women in particular often seem inhibited about talking about it or even trying it out. But masturbation is the best way to find out what you're into. After all, men like to have a partner who knows what she wants - even during sex. While it's perfectly legitimate to be unsure and not have figured out everything for y-ourself yet, getting to know your own body will also improve sex with your partner immensely.

Advantages of masturbation
• Intensive pelvic floor training
Strong pelvic floor muscles are important for health and prevent incontinence in old age. If they are neglected, the vagina's ability to tighten also

decreases. To counteract this, masturbation helps because it tenses the muscles, which strengthens them in the long term.

• Strengthening the immune system
Masturbation relaxes the body and consequently leads to improved sleep, which in turn strengthens the immune system. The happy hormones released during masturbation also reduce stress and can help prevent diseases such as depression or burnout.

• Period pain relief
For those who regularly suffer from pain during periods, masturbation offers a solution here as well. It has a relaxing effect and is also fun.

• Strengthening self-confidence
Doing something good for yourself boosts your self-confidence and is good for the soul. The time you take for yourself is insanely valuable and not only affects your physical health. If you know what you like, you can pass that knowledge on to your partner, who in turn will be happy to do something right.

MASTURBATION - THIS IS HOW IT WORKS

When, how often, where, how? Many questions can arise around the topic of masturbation. How you do it doesn't matter as long as you like it, but there are some methods and tips that have proven to work. Whether it's clitoral or vaginal stimulation, on your back or stomach, with toys or by hand, the possibilities are endless and offer a lot of room for experimentation. With a few basic tips, fun is guaranteed.

• Care for mood

To be able to relax properly and concentrate fully on yourself, you should create the right atmosphere. Find a place where you can be undisturbed, put on some music you like, and create a pleasant atmosphere by lighting some candles, for example. Preferences are quite individual, so see what you need to put yourself in the right mood.

• Watch porn

Porn may not be for everyone, but many people are into some visual stimulation. There are also more and more good alternatives to porn, which is otherwise very unrealistic and typically geared towards heterosexual men.

• Invest in sex toys

Vibrators in particular are something that are guaranteed to give most women an orgasm. They are great for when you want to relax and not do the work yourself. The selection from smaller to larger devices is incredibly diverse.

• Get to know your anatomy

Knowing your anatomy better will help you understand where you like to touch yourself or where you want your partner to touch you. For example, did you know that the clitoris is much more than the tip that is visible on the outside? More than 90% of the clitoris is located inside the body.

• Use lubricant

Lubricating gel is a good way to relieve the feeling of excessive irritation. Especially when you penetrate yourself, the gel is a good helper.

• Move your fingers in different ways

Whether circular or diagonal movements or a light tap - the possibilities are many.

• Try penetration

While clitoral stimulation pretty much provides the likelihood of an orgasm, this way it can be extended and intensified. Try it with your fingers or with a dildo to increase the fun even more.

• Try different positions

As with sex with a partner, you can also try out different positions on your own. On the back, on the stomach or on the side, sitting, standing or in the doggy position - try out what you like.

Friendship Plus

Not every relationship with a man always has to go straight to a committed relationship. Many people nowadays opt for a non-binding Friendship Plus, also called Friendship with Extras or Friends with Benefits. Here, two friends decide to have sex with each other occasionally, leaving out any romantic feelings. In this chapter, you'll learn about the advantages and disadvantages of this relationship model, the rules you should follow, and whether it's possible to turn a Friendship Plus into a committed relationship.

ADVANTAGES OF FRIENDSHIP PLUS

• You can maintain your freedom and independence and still have regular sex with someone you trust.

• Unlike committed relationships, a routine or boredom is less likely to set in.

• You feel less inhibited with a familiar friend than with a stranger.

• There is no feeling of obligation to have sex; it only takes place when both of you really feel like it.

• The feeling of being desired boosts your self-confidence.

DISADVANTAGES OF FRIENDSHIP PLUS

• If the Friendship Plus ends, it may also mean the end of your friendship.

• This relationship model lacks stability and security, which could make you feel insecure in the long run. The knowledge that, due to a lack of commitment, the relationship could soon be over, can be experienced as very stressful.

• Since it is unclear how long such a Friendship Plus will last, it is difficult to plan for the future.

• Unpleasant feelings such as jealousy may arise.

• Often a friendship plus ends because one of the two people has developed romantic feelings. This is usually accompanied by heartbreak.

THESE ARE THE RULES YOU SHOULD FOLLOW

While a Friendship Plus is a non-binding relationship and should be uncomplicated, it is for this very reason that it requires certain rules.

1. Discuss your boundaries.

You should first be aware of what you want and discuss it together. Is it okay for you if the other person has sex with other people? What about contraception? To avoid conflicts, it is absolutely necessary to clarify such questions in advance.

2. Communicate honestly with each other.

Honest communication is enormously important in any form of relationship, and Friendship Plus is no exception. In particular, if feelings arise or change in either party, you need to talk about it. Only with open and honest communication can you approach the matter in an uncomplicated way.

3. Avoids relationship-typical behavior.
In a Friendship Plus, behaviors like holding hands and cuddling, typical couple behavior, are taboo. Ideally, you should also sleep separately and refrain from making yourselves at home with each other. This would potentially only complicate your relationship unnecessarily.

4. No room for jealousy.
You can make individual agreements, but basically you cannot demand fidelity from the other person in a Friendship Plus. Do not give room to jealousy and do not reproach each other.

CAN YOU TURN A FRIENDSHIP PLUS INTO A COMMITTED RELATIONSHIP?

Before asking yourself if it is possible to turn a Friendship Plus into a committed relationship, you should instead ask yourself if you are comfortable with the Friendship Plus model. Are you okay with living with uncertainty and instability, but enjoying noncommittal sex? Also, are you okay with your partner being sexually active with other people? The chances that a noncommittal Friendship Plus can turn into a committed relationship are not completely bad, but it should not become the approach to a committed relationship. In many cases, such friendships end because romantic feelings arise on one side that cannot be reciprocated by the other.

Feelings can hardly be controlled. So it can happen quite unexpectedly that you find yourself in such a situation and realize that you have developed romantic feelings. But all is not lost yet.

First, take a critical look at your relationship. How often do you see each other? Rather rarely or does he even take you to friends' houses occasionally? Does he show interest now and then or is your relationship rather distant? If you can somewhat assess the current situation between you, it will also be easier for you to assess how realistic it is that more could develop between you. If your meetings sometimes feel like dates and you have deep conversations, this may indicate that he is also open to something more permanent.

Also, make sure you meet more often. The more often you see each other, the more likely it is that a deeper connection will develop between you. Speaking of connection: You should show interest by asking questions that will bring you closer emotionally. You can ask him questions about his childhood, his goals and dreams that will show him that you are genuinely interested in him as a person and that you value him.

What is at least as important is that you also value yourself. Only someone who is convinced of himself can manage to convince others of himself. So instead of belittling yourself and idealizing him, think of reasons that make you a great partner. If you then manage to convey this positive attitude to the outside world, this charisma may also have a special effect on him. Also, don't forget to respect yourself and set a limit for yourself. This means that you should not run after him forever if he does not immediately respond to your attempts. For example, take a month to move things along and if it's still a fruitless attempt, have an honest talk.

That brings us to the point of honesty. Speaking out makes you vulnerable, but it also opens doors. From this point of view, you have nothing to lose, because your feelings will certainly not disappear overnight and continuing to have a friendship plus with him would only mean another torture for you. By being honest, there is a possibility that your wish will come true. However, one thing is clear: your Friendship Plus is already over from the point when one of the two people realizes that there is more there. It can either come down to a relationship or you going your separate ways again. Everything in between is not reasonable for anyone. For this reason, you should also expect that your plan may backfire and that he will not reciprocate your feelings. This is painful, but this feeling will also pass and all you have left at this moment is to move on. Even though there is no guarantee of success, trying to turn a Friendship Plus into a relationship can be worthwhile.

Long distance relationships

Long-distance relationships are a specialty among the various relationship models. Hardly anyone who has a serious interest in having a steady and long-term relationship would prefer a long-distance relationship to a "normal" relationship. But love falls where it falls, and it would be a shame to miss a great opportunity just because the distance is not right at the moment. The fact that the number of long-distance relationships is on the rise is probably due to the fact that online dating is becoming more and more widespread, automatically increasing the search radius. This brings pitfalls with it, such as the mostly undesirable long-distance relationships or the never-ending search for the perfect partner, as the possibilities seem endless. But despite all the difficulties that can exist with long-distance relationships, they are not fundamentally pointless.

Spending time together, in real life, is essential for any relationship. Therefore, you should also try to find time for each other as often as possible. If the distance allows it, you can see each other every weekend or at least every two weeks. If even that is not possible, good planning and possibly longer meetings are essential. If you can see each other at least a few days at a time, this will compensate for the waiting time in between. But no matter how often you can see each other in the end, spending everyday life together and developing a real "we" feeling is certainly not possible for the time being. Unfortunately, many long-distance relationships break up because of this, as some people can't cope with the constant longing and distance. In order for a long-distance relationship to still be a happy one, a positive change in thinking is required: a long-distance relationship is merely a current situation and is not meant to last. In fact, the average long-distance relationship lasts only two years, after which most couples either break up or bridge the distance and start living together.

For the chances of a happy ending to be good, however, something must be actively done about it. Contact by phone, video chat, text messages and letters are an integral part of long-distance relationships and - thanks to today's technology - are becoming increasingly easy to implement. While long-distance communication is no substitute for real meetings and genuine face-to-face communication, it definitely makes the situation more bearable and maintains closeness between you. Also, don't just seek contact with each other when you have something important to tell each other, because after all, it's also about sharing your everyday life with each other, even if it sometimes seems a bit mundane.

TIPS FOR A SUCCESSFUL LONG DISTANCE RELATIONSHIP

• Plan your future together.

Shared plans give your relationship perspective and meaning. It is not so important whether all these plans come true, what is important is that you dream together and have something to look forward to. Where do you want to live later and how? Do you want to have children? If so, what names do you want to give them? Do you want to keep a pet? In addition to such long-term plans, you should also have medium-term goals, such as joint travel and projects.

• Leverages technology.

Or rather, the communication possibilities that come with it. Text, make video calls, send voice memos. So much is possible today, and it makes contact immensely easier. But if we stay with long distance communication, nothing beats a personal message like in a letter or a small package where you give a gift of attention. This shows appreciation and arrives at the partner in a very special way.

• Develop fixed rituals.

Rituals give a relationship security and convey a sense of belonging between the partners. For example, you can wish each other good morning and good night every day, or cook and eat together via video chat. It is important that you are available for each other, even if you each have your own lives to lead. But despite the distance, such fixed rituals give you a sense of togetherness that can easily be lost in long-distance relationships.

• Agree on fixed rules to which you will adhere in a binding manner.

Commitment through agreements can strengthen the necessary trust in a long-distance relationship. Agreements also help you to arrive in this possibly unfamiliar form of relationship and to consolidate mutual reliability. This also means that both people should make an effort to actively maintain the relationship by always talking about open wishes, suggestions for improvement and needs.

• Remember moments together.

Sharing memories brings you closer together, creates stability and the feeling of knowing each other well. To always have something that re-minds you of your partner, you can start collecting photos, movie tickets, letters or souvenirs of common trips in an album or in a nice box.

ARE YOU SUITABLE FOR A LONG DISTANCE RELATIONSHIP?

Only you can decide whether you are made for a long-distance relationship. With the right partner, even this somewhat unpleasant transition period can be bridged well, but it's not always easy. If you then decide to finally live together, you may have to prepare yourself for one or two nasty surprises. It is therefore advisable to spend some time together beforehand in order to weigh up whether the individual lifestyles are really compatible. In any case, anyone who embarks on a long-distance relationship should have long-term intentions, be able to accept compromises and bring along some resilience.

Personality development

The greatest relationship is of no use to you if you can't get along with yourself. Or to put it another way, if you're not happy with yourself, it will be difficult to have a happy relationship. Personality development is a process that can last your whole life. At the very least, ideally, one's entire life is a learning process of getting to know oneself better and trying to improve oneself. However, one should not fall prey to self-improvement mania, but rather try to find one's own strengths in a healthy way and work on them to reach one's full

potential. Also, practice self-love in order to culti-
vate a fulfilling partnership as well.

SELF LOVE - LEARNING TO LOVE YOURSELF

Practicing a little more self-love sounds like a big task. But it's not that difficult to incorporate a few behaviors into your everyday life to gradually build up more love for yourself. With the following tips, you're sure to succeed!

1. Take time for yourself.
Even just half an hour that you take for yourself today can work wonders. When was the last time you really thought only about yourself? Thinking only about yourself for a moment has nothing to do with selfishness, but with true self-love.

2. Treat yourself to something good.
If you're already taking some time for yourself, you might as well treat yourself to something good. A visit to the sauna, a massage or a simple but soothing walk in the forest are balm for body and soul.

3. What are you grateful for?
Practicing gratitude is an insanely effective tool on the path to greater self-love. It is a good exercise to do in the evening. The best way to do this is to write down what you are grateful for in yourself and in your environment, your fellow human beings. It doesn't have to be anything earth-shattering, because sometimes even the most banal things are enough to make us feel more appreciation and gratitude.

4. Treat yourself like a best friend.
Best friends want only the best for each other. If you transfer this attitude to your own self, you are a big step closer to self-love.

5. Forgive yourself.
You know those moments when a bad memory comes up out of nowhere and you feel bad for something you failed at? Let go of the past and don't dwell on it. Forgive yourself for any mistakes you may have made. Past is past, mistakes are there to learn from them and to forgive yourself again.

6. Be patient with yourself.

Not everything in life has to work out right away. Patience pays off and will get you further than giving up or putting yourself down because of failures. Don't take life too seriously in this process, but focus on the good and have the confidence that with patience everything will work out.

7. Smile.

Even when you don't feel like it, it can do you good to simply put on a smile. You'll notice that your smile, which may still be artificial at first, has a positive effect on your mood, and you'll radiate this to the outside world as well.

8. Be proud of your accomplishments.

Take the time to celebrate your successes and achievements. Especially things you didn't think you could accomplish for a long time deserve their own pride.

9. Show love for your fellow man.

Even though we are talking about self-love here, love for your fellow human beings should not be underestimated. We're not just talking about your partner, your family or your friends, but also strangers or people you don't like at all. Accepting them all as they are and taking a new perspective can have a very healing effect on your own self-image, because often the devaluation of other people is related to a poor self-image.

DEAL WITH ENERGY VAMPIRES

We call people energy vampires who literally drain our energy in everyday life, for example by talking badly about others or criticizing us all the time. Almost everyone will certainly know such people in their environment, just like the feeling of being drained after an encounter with them. Not only distant acquaintances or people with whom we are forced to be in contact can drain our energy. Friends, family members or our own partner can also become energy vampires. With the negativity they radiate, they cause damage, which is why you should ideally avoid them.

How do you recognize people who rob you of your strength?

Analyze your environment and ask yourself the following questions:
- Is this person just thinking of his own advantage and wants to take advantage of my helpfulness?
- Am I getting less out of this relationship with this person than I am investing in it myself?
- Does this person not accept my goals and instead dictate how I should live?

If you can answer "yes" to these questions, you are probably dealing with an energy vampire.

What you can do against energy vampires

If you find that you have an energy vampire in your life, you will certainly notice how it negatively affects your mood. Continuous pessimism is out of place on your path of personality development. So do something in time against annoying energy suckers.

• Set clear boundaries.

• Draw attention to your own needs when the conversation is once again all about the other person.

• Be aware of your own desires and be guided only by them.

• Surround yourself with positive people who mean well and want to support you.

WORK ON YOUR STRENGTHS

From an early age, it is drummed into us that we need to work on our weak points. For example, if a child was bad at math, he or she should do math and solve more problems to get better. Even in adulthood, many people are still intent on trying to compensate for their weaknesses, even though this is actually a hindrance to reaching our full potential. Compensating for our weaknesses can, at best, make us average. It is rarely the case that one of our personal weaknesses suddenly becomes a strength. How could it? After all, our natural talents provide the ideal foundation to continue building on them and become true experts in these areas. Focusing on your weaknesses is usually a waste of time, as working on your strengths is so much easier and more fun. This can be applied to just about any personality trait or skill. A quote from Albert Einstein illustrates this situation a bit better: "Everyone is a genius. But if you judge a fish by its ability to climb a tree, it will think it's stupid all its life."

ALLOW CHANGE

Wanting to develop one's own personality will inevitably have to mean perhaps doing certain things differently. However, change, of any kind, can sometimes be quite scary. You're leaving familiar territory, familiar patterns of behavior and thought, and you're forced to get used to something new. Wanting to change something is therefore quite often a somewhat uncomfortable thing, but change also means further development and room for improvement. If you never want to change anything in your life, you will miss the chance for positive development and you will stay at the same point forever. This can be very frustrating in the long run and cause dissatisfaction.

What to do about the fear of change?
The world is in a constant state of change, just like your very own world. Nothing stays the way it is now forever. Our fellow human beings and the environment are constantly changing, which is hard to digest for some from time to time, but a certain fear towards change is normal and nothing reprehensible. However, it feels insanely liberating to let go of the old, break through old dependencies and be ready to move forward.

Maybe you sometimes feel that your heart is crying out for change, but you just don't dare to do anything radically different. It is true that every change brings a risk with it, but at the same time there is also a huge opportunity in it. Have you always wanted to go on a trip around the world, have the necessary means and know a way to do it, but just don't dare yet? Let go of your fears and at the same time get involved in something new, just try it. Even if you find that a change in your life was not the right one after all, you can always return to the previous state, that is, if it is really irreversible change.

A second way to combat the fear of change is to feel your inner child more strongly again. You need the child inside you to know again what you really need to be happy. Children are usually passionate, curious, take on challenges and are fully themselves. Focusing on this part of your personality can help you figure out what it is you want to change in the first place. The intuitive child in you usually knows best.

At the same time, you should not neglect the adult side of yourself, but don't confuse it with a critic who is too strict. The adult part, on the other hand, should help you to objectively assess current situations to see if the conflicts you are carrying around are really as hopeless as they seem to you. The risks or what you could potentially lose are not as present as we often make them out to be. To become really aware of this, you can write down arguments and think about them better.

GET OUT OF YOUR COMFORT ZONE

Everyone has their own comfort zone. It offers you safety and security and, above all, support when things go haywire in other areas of life. But staying trapped in your comfort zone forever is not a desirable goal, because you can't develop or grow beyond yourself within this comfort zone.

This zone includes everything you feel secure in and what you already know: Hobbies, friends, thought patterns, and so on. These are all things that have worked for you over the years, but at the same time you are severely limiting yourself if you never go beyond them. In very mundane terms, if you only ever order the same dish in a restaurant, you miss out on enjoying all the other dishes. If you always wear the same clothes, you don't know how great it can feel to wear something different. If you stay in your old ways of thinking, you miss the opportunity to grow as a person.

This is what you have to win

When you step out of your comfort zone, you have the opportunity to gain new experiences and try new things. If you go just a little bit beyond your own limits, you have already developed further, and that is a great feeling in retrospect. Of course, there may also be unpleasant experiences, but even these insights will take you further, because they make you more self-confident and shape your image of who you are and what you want.

In addition to good experiences, you'll have the opportunity for more positive feelings. While stepping out of your comfort zone can feel very scary at first, you will be rewarded in the end and eventually the positive feelings will outweigh the negative ones. When you leave the familiar, you can gain a lot of fun, self-confidence, and self-esteem while discovering sides of yourself that you didn't even know existed before.

In addition, leaving your comfort zone means more self-determination for you. You set yourself free from other people's expectations and free from beliefs and thought patterns that you yourself are stuck in. You are the one who determines your own life! However, the inner critic in us can sometimes get quite loud. Especially when certain events that challenge us are approaching, you have to muster all your courage to implement the plan anyway. Listening beyond your own self-doubt is usually very difficult in these situations, but it is for this very reason that you need to shut down your inner critic and dare to try something new.

How to get out of your comfort zone
• What is the worst-case scenario?
The scenarios that arise in your head when you approach a challenge resemble a horror movie? This feeling is very common, but in virtually all cases unnecessary. Instead, think about what could realistically happen in the worst case scenario. In the vast majority of cases, it really isn't dramatic. Life goes on afterwards.

• What about the best-case scenario?
And now think: What can happen in the best case? Just the thought of the feelings of happiness and pride you can feel for yourself afterwards will

surely be reason enough to accept the challenge. The sweet feeling of success will nullify and forget your previous fears as well as expand your comfort zone bit by bit.

• Be specific about what you want to do.
In order not to shirk anything and not to make excuses, it is necessary that you start to specify in writing what you want to achieve. To do this, you can write everything that belongs to your comfort zone in a circle on a sheet of paper. Outside the circle, write down things that you haven't dared to do yet, but that you think will move your life forward. Take two or three of the things outside the circle and formulate specific sentences. Phrase these sentences with "I will" and ideally set a deadline or goal for how often you will do something.

• Involve other people in your project.
In order to achieve your goals, it is very important that you commit yourself to them. Even if it is rather irrelevant what other people think, it can be helpful to let them in on your plans. By making a promise to others, you have little choice but to put your best foot forward. In addition, you may

find someone who will support you and, in turn, you can help them achieve their goals.

• Just do it!
Uncomfortable feelings when leaving your comfort zone are completely normal and by no means a sign to stop now. Rather, they signal to you that you're right on track. So instead of giving up at these moments, remind yourself to just embrace these feelings. They will quickly pass and before long turn into a feeling of relief and satisfaction with yourself.

• Celebrate yourself.
No matter how small the step you took was, it's important to pat yourself on the back and reward yourself afterwards.

• Reflect on yourself.
Last but not least, think about how it felt to leave your comfort zone and what you can take away from it. What helped you to triumph over your inner bastard? What can you learn from it?

With all these tips, don't forget to be patient with yourself and don't give up immediately if something doesn't work out right away. Take small steps and keep questioning your self-image. Maybe you have already come much further than you think?

BE HAPPY EVEN WITHOUT A PARTNER

While this is a guide to help you meet men, find a partner, and have happy relationships, the basis of it all is ultimately always your own sense of satisfaction. No partner in the world will be able to help you if you are dead unhappy with all other areas of your life. And desperately clinging to the idea that with the right man by your side everything will be fine shouldn't be your goal either. Instead, make it your goal to be happy without a partner. Everything that comes after that is a bonus that can only enrich your life. How you can be happy without a partner, you will learn in the following briefly summarized.

1. Be good to yourself.

With all your tasks and obligations, it is important that you do not lose sight of taking care of yourself. Treat yourself regularly, be a little selfish when it comes to your deepest needs and desires. For example, one day a week you can resolve to do something special, whether it's a little spa day at home, an evening with friends and cocktails, or a walk in the woods in the fresh air.

2. Discover your passion.

Everyone needs some kind of purpose in life. Passions, interests and hobbies are usually what motivate and drive people, and you should have a passion like that too. It doesn't matter what it is, as long as you are passionate about it and it gives you a sense of fulfillment.

3. Do sports.

Exercise has numerous benefits for your physical as well as mental health. Whether you're a sports slacker or someone who likes to be on the move all the time: Trying new sports is worth it. You can set specific goals and observe your own successes over time, giving you a better body image and self-image.

4. Take care of your health.
Taking care of your health is essential for a happy and long life. In addition to adequate exercise, you should pay attention to your diet, stress levels and good sleep. Such tips may already be hanging out of your ears, but if you take a closer look, you may realize that you don't sleep well enough or eat consciously after all. It can actually be really fun to pay attention to such things, and you'll also notice that you feel much better over time.

5. Change your appearance.
If you want to change something in your life for the better, an external change can accompany you. Have you wanted to try out a different hairstyle for a long time, but haven't dared yet? Do you want to get a tattoo or piercing? Try out new clothes? Whatever it is, dare to do what makes you happy.

6. Nurture your friendships.

Being able to meet and exchange ideas with other people is enormously important for a good quality of life. So take good care of your existing friendships, but also try to expand your circle of friends. The more your self-confidence grows, the more you will dare to approach new people and make friends.

7. Realize your professional dreams.

The job with which we finance our lives usually takes up a lot of our valuable life time. For this reason, it is especially important that you are satisfied with your professional life. Make your dreams concrete and think about what you need to do to achieve them.

8. Put yourself out there for a good cause.

Advocating for charitable causes can become a new passion. What is close to your heart? What would you like to change in this society? Would you like to do something for animals in shelters or for the homeless? Maybe donate to an organization? There are many possibilities and maybe you will find something you would like to do.

9. Go on a journey.

It doesn't matter if it's just a short trip to a big city not far away or a whole trip around the world: Traveling enriches and advances your personal development. Especially when you travel alone, you get to know yourself and possibly other cultures and people.

10. Do it for you.

You can do all the tips listed here - but do them for yourself and not because you secretly want to impress a man. In the end, you should only look for a partner that suits you, not one that you adapt to. In your self-discovery process you will find out what you actually need and want, also in a partnership. If everything then comes together in a harmonious way, with or without a partner, you can lead a truly happy life.

Where do we go from here?

In this guide you have learned a lot about men, partnerships and the development of their own personality. But ultimately there is no universal recipe for anything and not every man ticks the same. This guide is intended to give you some basic food for thought and, above all, to show you that it really isn't witchcraft to get to know men and find the right partner for you among them.

Now it's your turn to put your goals into action. This can sometimes require a lot of strength and perseverance, but it will be worth it. I wish you success in everything! You will make it!

Thank you!

Thank you so much for choosing to purchase this book. I hope it has helped you and I wish you all the best in your future endeavors!